THE RED PORSCHE

(you're worth it!)

[& OTHER TOPICS FOR **LDS YOUTH**]

DAVID J. RIDGES

THE RED PORSCHE

(you're worth it!)

[& OTHER TOPICS FOR **LDS YOUTH**]

DAVID J. RIDGES

CFI
AN IMPRINT OF CEDAR FORT, INC.
SPRINGVILLE, UTAH

ISBN 13: 978-1-4621-1786-4

Published by CFI, an imprint of Cedar Fort, Inc., 2373 W. 700 S., Springville, UT 84663
Distributed by Cedar Fort, Inc., www.cedarfort.com

LIBRARY OF CONGRESS CATALOGING-IN-PUBLICATION DATA

Names: Ridges, David J., author.
Title: The red Porsche : and other topics for LDS youth / David J. Ridges.
Description: Springville, Utah : CFI, An imprint of Cedar Fort, Inc., [2016] | Includes bibliographical references and index.
Identifiers: LCCN 2016024429 (print) | LCCN 2016027849 (ebook) | ISBN 9781462117864 (perfect bound : alk. paper) | ISBN 9781462125937 (epub, pdf, mobi)
Subjects: LCSH: Mormon youth--Conduct of life.
Classification: LCC BX8643.Y6 R53 2016 (print) | LCC BX8643.Y6 (ebook) | DDC 248.4/89332--dc23
LC record available at https://lccn.loc.gov/2016024429

Cover design by Shawnda T. Craig

Edited and typeset by Heather Holm
Interior design by Rebecca Bird and Heather Holm

Printed in the United States of America

10 9 8 7 6 5 4 3 2 1

Printed on acid-free paper

Dedicated to the thousands of amazing youth of the Church whom I have been privileged to teach over many years, and to those who are yet coming, who strive so faithfully to carry the banner of the gospel throughout the world.

Books by David J. Ridges

The Gospel Studies Series

- *Isaiah Made Easier, Second Edition*
- *The New Testament Made Easier, Parts 1–2 (Second Edition)*
- *Your Study of The Book of Mormon Made Easier, Parts 1–3*
- *Your Study of The Doctrine and Covenants Made Easier, Parts 1–3*
- *The Old Testament Made Easier—Parts 1–3*
- *Your Study of the Pearl of Great Price Made Easier*
- *Your Study of Jeremiah Made Easier*
- *Your Study of The Book of Revelation Made Easier, Second Edition*
- *Scriptures Made Easier Family Deluxe Editions*

Additional Titles

- *Our Savior, Jesus Christ: His Life and Mission to Cleanse and Heal*
- *Mormon Beliefs and Doctrines Made Easier*
- *The Proclamation on the Family: The Word of the Lord on More Than 30 Current Issues*
- *65 Signs of the Times and the Second Coming*
- *Doctrinal Details of the Plan of Salvation: From Premortality to Exaltation*
- *Using the Signs of the Times to Strengthen Your Testimony*
- *A Mother's Perfect Hope*
- *Priesthood Power Unlocked*
- *Unlocking the Power of Your Priesthood*
- *Temples: Sacred Symbolism, Eternal Blessings*
- *Born to the Virgin Mary*
- *The Righteous Role of the Father*
- *The Red Porsche*

CONTENTS

1

THE RED PORSCHE

You're Worth It!

What we think of ourselves plays an important role in whether or not we repent quickly and thoroughly when we slip up. If we respect ourselves and feel we are worth repairing, we tend to act quickly and take care of it through repentance. However, if we feel that we are not valuable or worth it, perhaps thinking that we have too many areas in our lives where we are lacking as followers of Christ, we may not feel any particular urgency about getting our lives back in order.

Porsche makes several different lines of high performance automobiles. Some years ago, a wealthy friend of mine heard that the company was manufacturing a limited edition of a high-performance Porsche slant-nose turbo sports car. They were limiting the production run to one hundred of them. Excited, he immediately phoned company headquarters in Germany to order one. But it was too late. All one hundred had been presold.

My friend was a highly successful businessman and manufacturer. To go along with it, he was second to none as a salesman. The more he thought about it, the more passionate he became about doing all he could to acquire one. He tried several approaches but was unsuccessful in convincing the company to do an end run around the stated limit of one hundred. Ultimately, he exercised all his persuasive skills as a salesman and finally talked a high company official of Porsche into producing one more.

The high purchase price of the coveted vehicle included special driving lessons on a high-speed test track in Germany to prepare drivers to take full advantage of the machine's incredible capabilities, as well as to prevent premature death behind the wheel. While waiting for his car to be built, my friend flew to Germany and took the driving lessons. He returned home and carpeted one side of his garage for his soon-to-be treasured Porsche. He also added floodlights to his garage to shine on it when it arrived.

He arranged in advance to have the gorgeous, deep red, candy apple-colored sports car air freighted from Germany to New York as soon as it came off the assembly line. As that day approached, he excitedly told me about it and promised to give me a ride as soon as he arrived home with it in Springville, Utah. He lived just a couple of blocks from our home. As he chatted with me, he also disclosed that he had made a small bet with his wife that he could drive it from the airport in New York to Springville in less than two days. He won, driving the distance in just under twenty-seven hours! He averaged over one hundred miles per hour, allowing for a few brief naps and stops along the way. I chided him a bit for breaking the posted speed limits and joked that he should have surrendered his temple recommend to the bishop before going. He grinned.

Soon after he arrived home and spent some time with his wife and family, I heard the deep rumble of the powerful, turbo-charged Porsche engine alongside the curb in front of our home. I looked out the window, and, sure enough, he was there, as promised, to give me a ride. I had been working in the garage and had greasy clothes on, so I went to the front door and signaled him that I would be right out after I changed. Quickly, I washed my hands, dressed in a clean shirt, slacks, and shoes, and went out and walked slowly around the dream machine, absorbing the magnificent lines and admiring the deep, mirror-like layers of clear coat that highlighted the beauty of the paint. I looked inside and saw that it had beautiful white kid-glove leather upholstery.

As I opened the passenger door to get in, he stopped me. "Dave," he said, "let me tell you how to get in." I stopped. He instructed me to turn around, facing away from the car, and back up to the side of the seat. With both feet still on the ground, I was to lower myself into the car and lift both of my feet high above the car threshold. Then I was to carefully pivot my body and place both my feet on the floor mat, without dragging them at all to scratch the threshold. I carefully complied.

Fastening my seat belt, I was ready to go! He showed me the instrument panel with lights that lit up as rpms and speed increased. I was thrilled! He described the engine features. He told me that the tires were made of a special gummy tread material for traction since ordinary tires would merely spin against the road and screech and smoke when full power was applied. He mentioned that such tires have a rather short useful life and cost about two thousand dollars each to replace.

He drove carefully through town and took us to a seldom-used road west of town. There he stopped. He grinned and asked if I was ready. I said, "Yes." We went from zero to sixty miles per hour and back to zero in less than six seconds! I was sure I had flat spots on the back of my eyeballs for several days thereafter. It was amazing and thrilling! He even came over to our home a few weeks later and gave each of our older children short rides in the Porsche for family night. They were likewise thrilled.

The owner obviously took meticulous care of the Porsche. I often grinned when I saw it parked at the Provo Temple, always in a parallel parking space where it would not be damaged by having a door opened into it. At church, my friend parked slantwise in two normal parking spaces—again, to avoid getting a door dinged.

Some months went by, and my friend was driving at night to a second home he and his wife had in a nice area of Park City, Utah, a little more than an hour's drive from Springville. It was a dark night on a mountain highway, and he hit a deer. It damaged a front fender and sent the deer to whatever spirit world arrangements await deer and other animals and creatures that have finished their mortal existence. My friend was not injured, but he was mortified! His new, beautiful, expensive, rare, and much-loved Porsche had hit a deer! When he told me about it, I wondered what the deer had said to his fellow expired deer in the spirit world as they chatted about how they had died. I can hear him bragging to his colleagues, "I took out a red Porsche! You should have seen the guy's face as I hit his car!" (I'm just imagining this, of course!)

There was no question about fixing the damage. The car was far more than worth it. A new front fender was ordered from the factory. It cost about two thousand dollars for a relatively small fender, primed and ready to be installed and painted to match the rest of the vehicle. The best available body and fender shop expert was hired to make the repair. When my friend showed it to me after the repair, it was impossible to tell that it had ever been damaged. It was as good as new! It was absolutely worth repairing! My friend's enjoyment of his fabulous, exotic car continued.

Then, one day, he told me that he had sold his Porsche. I was stunned. I asked why. His answer was simple. He told me of pulling up beside an older car at a stoplight downtown. He looked over at the driver and thought, *That poor slob, being stuck with that miserable excuse for transportation. I'll bet he's jealous of me.* The light changed, and, showing off a bit, he made sure he quickly left the other fellow behind. As he later told me about this, he said that as he drove on, he realized that his heart had become set on his riches, and the Porsche was corrupting his soul. Facing this realization, he promptly sold it.

In the scriptures, we are taught of the infinite worth of each of our souls as children of Heavenly Parents. We are also taught of the great joy it brings to the Savior when we accept His gift of repentance and being forgiven.

<u>D&C 18:10–13</u>

10 Remember **the worth of souls is great** in the sight of God;

11 For, behold, the Lord **your Redeemer** suffered death in the flesh; wherefore he **suffered the pain of all men, that all men might repent and come unto him**.

12 And he hath risen again from the dead, that he might bring all men unto him, on conditions of repentance.

13 And **how great is his joy in the soul that repenteth!**

The account of the red Porsche is given here to remind you of the importance of repenting quickly and thoroughly when you slip up on keeping the commandments of God. After the accident with the deer, there was no question as to whether or not it was worth fixing. Likewise, there is no question in the Savior's mind as to whether or not we are worth repairing. That is what His Atonement is all about. And it works perfectly! We become new creatures in Christ (2 Corinthians 5:17). In other words, we can start over, literally, and are new people, and our sins will not be brought up on judgment day (D&C 58:42).

But it all depends on if we are willing to exercise our agency to access the Atonement through repentance.

Over many years as a seminary and institute teacher, as well as serving as a bishop and stake president, I found that several things can stand in the way of getting our "dings" and "dents," so to speak, repaired by the Atonement of Christ. A major one is to procrastinate repenting. It can be described by the story of another nice automobile. This time, the car belonged to me.

It wasn't a brand new car, but it was a top-of-the-line, beautiful, silver-gray Chrysler LeBaron Medallion with a powerful engine. It had gray leather upholstery and was in beautiful condition. We had to replace one of our family's cars because of an unfortunate, unplanned meeting of it with a light pole on a slick winter road. The reason the Chrysler was within our budget was that the engine had a rough idle that had evaded the efforts of several mechanics to remedy. Having worked somewhat as a mechanic myself, during and after college, I fancied I could fix it, so we bought it.

After several unsuccessful attempts at solving the problem of the rough idle, including removing the top of the engine and installing new intake manifold gaskets, as well as checking and rechecking the fuel system, I finally found the problem and fixed it. It ran beautifully. I, too, parked in parallel parking spaces where possible to avoid door dings. When we went to stores, I intentionally parked far out in the parking lots where there were few if any other cars so I could admire the shiny car from a distance as I walked back to it after shopping. I washed and waxed it often. In winter driving conditions, where a lot of road salt was used, I occasionally found small pinpoint rust spots on the body. I faithfully buffed out the tiny spots.

Then one day I came out to the parking lot and found a five-inch-long, shallow but noticeable, green gouge on the driver's door where someone in a green car had parked to the side of me. He had obviously swung the passenger door of his car clear open and made contact with my Chrysler. He was gone. I was sick. I looked for a note on my windshield, hoping that maybe he was a person of integrity and had left contact information, but there was none. Rather than fixing it right away, I let it go, thinking I would take care of it soon.

As time went on, small rust spots appeared, especially during winter driving. Rather than immediately buffing them out, as had been my practice in the past, I let them go, planning on taking care of them later, perhaps in the spring or summer. The green smudge still graced the driver's door, but it no longer caught my eye. I was used to having it there. Then one day, I was exiting the freeway to attend a meeting in Salt Lake City. As I slowed for the stopped traffic at the light at the bottom of the ramp, which filled all lanes, I glanced in my rearview mirror and gasped. A car some distance behind me was coming toward me at full speed. The driver was obviously distracted and had not yet applied the brakes. I tried to pull off to the left, but there was no room. Too late! She hit the brakes and zigzagged in a screeching, futile attempt to stop. I watched the panicked look on her face in my rearview mirror and braced for the impact. Bang! Fortunately, she had slowed down a lot so that the damage was limited to my rear bumper, trunk, and taillights. She was protected by her airbag.

The police came and did the necessary paperwork. I was sad to see my beautiful car damaged, but I knew that a body shop could restore it. I contacted my insurance company, and they directed me to get bids for the repairs.

When the Chrysler came out of the shop, I carefully inspected the work and noticed that some of it was not well done. I could have requested that it be redone, but I was extremely busy at the time and decided I could live with it. After I made that decision, I noticed a subtle change in my feelings about my Chrysler LeBaron. I didn't value it as much. I began letting other things go. I didn't wash and wax it as often. I didn't clean the interior. I maintained it mechanically, but I didn't do much for it cosmetically.

Years went by, and my wife and I let our daughter use it for her transportation needs. One day when I got home from work, she told me that the car wouldn't make it up the short hill from our home as she drove to her classes at BYU. The engine was running but the car wouldn't climb the short hill. She had to back up, turn around, go down the hill, and take another route to campus. By then, I suppose it was warmed up enough that it got her there, on mostly level roads. I asked her if she had checked the transmission fluid recently. She replied, "What's that?" Turns out it was way low on transmission fluid. We filled it, and I gave her a quick lesson on checking the oil, transmission fluid, and antifreeze on a monthly basis. I reluctantly scolded myself for not caring enough about the once-beautiful car to make sure that at least the basics of maintenance were taken care of. Ultimately, the Chrysler died and was sold for the price of salvage at a local scrap yard.

As you can see, important lessons can be learned when considering the Red Porsche and the Chrysler. If you maintain a high sense of your eternal worth and your great potential as a son or daughter of God, you will tend to repent quickly as needed. The Atonement of Christ is constantly available when you get dings and dents in daily living. And, as you do repent quickly and sincerely, you will realize more and more that you are indeed worth it! The Holy Ghost will constantly confirm this celestial fact deep inside you, and your countenance will increasingly radiate the magnificence of the eternal soul that is the real you.

On the other hand, if you resign yourself to sin and lose vision of who you really are, you might mirror the path of the Chrysler, when daily care and maintenance gradually slowed down or stopped, and find yourself drifting farther and farther away from the deep joys and satisfactions found in living a gospel life.

Remember the beautiful and encouraging invitation from the Savior that is found in Isaiah.

> Isaiah 1:18
>
> 18 Come now, and let us reason together, saith the LORD: **though your sins be as scarlet, they shall be as white as snow**; though they be red like crimson, they shall be as wool.

By the way, did you know that *scarlet*, as used in the verse quoted above, was one of very few colorfast dyes available for use in fabrics in Isaiah's day? Such dyes resisted fading when washed and laundered. With that in mind, Isaiah 1:18 has added meaning for us. In effect, the

Lord is telling us that even if we think our sins are "colorfast" and can't be cleansed by His Atonement, we should think again. His Atonement can indeed remove our sins and transform our lives so that we are new people, clean and pure, with a wonderfully bright future!

In conclusion, repent quickly! You are worth it!

2

RECOGNIZING INSPIRATION

One of the most vital spiritual skills for you to learn in your youth is that of recognizing inspiration. The Spirit speaks to us in a variety of ways, including through thoughts, feelings, impressions, peace, dreams, visions, the words of parents and leaders, the scriptures, and more. Obviously, it is important that we recognize when the Lord is guiding our thoughts and actions through the Holy Ghost.

We are given a marvelous promise each week as we partake of the sacrament. It is found at the end of the sacrament prayer for the bread; namely, "that they may always have his Spirit to be with them" (D&C 20:77). What a promise! We can have His Spirit with us always! But what if we fail to recognize it when He is inspiring us? Let's look at some common ways that inspiration can come so you can watch for them in your daily life. Obviously, inspiration and revelation can be given to us in many ways. One of the most important things you can do is figure out what ways the Lord uses best to communicate with you.

SUDDEN THOUGHTS

"Those Were His Trees"

On a particularly memorable day some years ago, I was in the middle of teaching a rather spiritual portion of a seminary lesson. Two girls near the front of the class, who were normally attentive and excellent students, were incessantly whispering back and forth in a quiet but lively manner. Finally, I stopped, looked at them, smiled, and asked if they would mind holding their conversation until after class. They both flushed with embarrassment and apologized, promising to join in the lesson, which they did—for about three minutes. Soon, they were back at it. I again smiled and asked if they would mind holding their obviously exciting discussion until later. Again, they apologized and paid attention to class—this time for about two minutes.

As I mentioned, above, they were good students, and this was far from normal behavior for them. So I grinned at them and invited them to move to the back of the room. A couple of empty desks were against the wall, where the girls could finish whispering their impossible-to-suppress agenda and then rejoin the class. Blushing, they at first promised to be good, but then they looked at each other and simultaneously said, "Okay, we'll go back, but we'll whisper very quietly," which they did.

I continued the lesson. True to their promise, we could not hear their conversation. I could see their animated facial expressions and read their lips as they said, "Really!" and "No way!" back and forth, but soon, I successfully ignored them. A bit later in the lesson, as I turned around to write something on the board, with my back to the class, the words "Tell them 'those were his trees' " came clearly into my mind. It startled me! It was completely unrelated to the lesson and was the farthest possible thing from my mind.

I hesitated briefly and then turned around. I looked at them and said, "Girls, those were his trees." Their jaws dropped. Their eyes grew wide. They paled, and one of them said, "Brother Ridges, how did you know what we were talking about?" I confessed that I had no idea what they were discussing and responded, "I'm curious. Would you mind telling me what you were talking about?" to which they both replied, "No way!" But then one of them immediately said to the other, "We better tell him. He's getting revelation!"

Short story shorter, they had been gossiping about the bishop, who had just cut down several trees alongside the road past his house and pasture. The girls thought the trees were on city property and were indignant that he had cut them down. As it turned out, they were on his private property and were so tall that they were shading large portions of his pasture, which was keeping the grass there from growing well. Needless to say, the girls never chatted during class again.

Since then, I have often thought back on the incident with appreciation for "sudden thoughts" as a common means of communication by the Spirit. I've had them on occasions since then and observed that they often come when my mind is on something else entirely, not related to the subject of my thoughts. In fact, I believe that the very idea that sudden thoughts often come "out of the blue," so to speak, is, in itself, a clue that they are inspiration from God.

I remember hearing a story about Harold B. Lee, the President of the Church at the time, who was on a plane with several General Authorities, flying to an area conference. In the middle of a casual conversation during the flight, the Prophet suddenly stopped talking, pulled out notepaper, and jotted down some words. Smiling, he looked at the others, who had also stopped talking and remained silent. He told them, in effect, "Brethren, I was praying this morning in my office on an important matter before leaving for the airport. The answer did not come at that time. But just now, it came, so I stopped and wrote it down. I have learned that sudden thoughts are one way the Lord communicates His will to us."

President Harold B. Lee taught this later in a talk. He said,

> When there come to you things that your mind does not know, **when you have a sudden thought that comes to your mind**, if you will learn to give heed to these things that come from the Lord you will learn to walk by the spirit of revelation. (Area Conference Report [Mexico City, 1972], p. 49)

Joseph Smith also spoke of the importance of sudden thoughts when it comes to recognizing inspiration. He said,

> A person may profit by noticing the first intimation of the spirit of revelation; for instance, when you feel pure intelligence flowing into you, it may give you **sudden strokes of ideas**, so that by noticing it, you may find it fulfilled the same day or soon . . . and thus by learning the Spirit of God and understanding it, you may grow into

> the principle of revelation, until you become perfect in Christ Jesus. (*Teachings of the Prophet Joseph Smith* [Salt Lake City: Deseret Book, 1959], p. 151)

Often, a sudden thought might come into your mind to call or text someone with an encouraging word. Or you might have the impression to visit someone, slow down in your car, wait longer before starting on a green light at an intersection, hold off on speaking in anger to someone, say your morning prayer, turn down a date or accept a date, tell your mother you love her, or check the fuel gauge in the car. The list is endless. The basic idea with such thoughts is that they are often unexpected but carry important inspiration for a specific situation.

THE "DRY MORMON"

Faithful but Not Baptized

Years ago, we had what my seminary students affectionately called a "dry Mormon" (one who is living the gospel but has not yet been baptized) in one of my classes. He wanted to join the Church, but his father was dead set against it. The young man determined to live the gospel faithfully so that when he turned eighteen and could be baptized without his father's permission, he would already be active in the Church.

One Friday afternoon, during deer hunting season, he stayed after class until all the other students were gone and asked if he could chat with me. He told me that his father had invited him to go deer hunting the coming Sunday. He was conflicted. He told me his relationship with his father had been cool, and this was perhaps a chance for them to draw closer together. However, he said, it might be that his father was testing his commitment to living the standards of the Mormon Church. He asked for advice. I started to tell him that I thought it might be a test and that it would probably be best if he did not go hunting on Sunday. But, part way through my reply, a strong impression suddenly entered my mind, instructing me to tell him to go hunting with his father. I did so. It startled us both.

He followed that council, and on Monday, he excitedly told the class and me that his father had given him written permission to be baptized! As he told it, it seems that all day Sunday during the hunt, the Lord had protected all the deer from them. Consequently, they had a lot of time to chat and grow close together. Finally, at the end of the day, his father asked him to hand him the unused deer tag. He took a pencil and scrawled a brief note on the back of the tag, giving his son permission to be baptized. He was ecstatic! It was a glorious baptism and confirmation, attended by a large number of seminary students and friends. The "sudden thoughts" that came into my mind the previous Friday had now borne wonderful fruit.

THINGS THAT "PRESS UPON" YOUR MIND

The White Corvette Roof

A fairly common way that inspiration comes is when the Spirit places something in your mind and keeps it there until you respond. Joseph Smith referred to this type of inspiration as something that "presses upon" your mind. He mentioned it as he prepared to teach the early members of the Church more about baptism for the dead.

> D&C 128:1
>
> I now resume the subject of the baptism for the dead, as **that subject seems to occupy my mind, and press itself upon my feelings the strongest.**

During my days of coursework at a nearby university, I found it necessary to take full-time employment every summer to supplement my part-time job the rest of the year. During two of those summers, a friend and I took our young families to Wyoming where we worked cutting timber about thirty-five miles east of Jackson. After we harvested the usable trees for the sawmill, we clear-cut the remaining trees, and the Forest Service replanted the area. The nature of the work of a lumberjack involves a higher-than-average degree of physical danger. Therefore, the boss always required that we work in pairs in case one of us got into trouble.

During one summer, my friend had to return to Salt Lake City for two weeks to take care of school business. That left me without a cutting partner, so I contacted a friend named Bill and asked if he would like to spend two weeks in Wyoming cutting timber. He jumped at the chance. It would be high adventure for him. We had a glorious time, sometimes rather exciting when trees misbehaved. The days flew by, and soon it was time for Bill and his wife to return home to Salt Lake. He later told me what happened as they drove home late at night after his final day of hard work in the timber.

He said he was having a hard time staying awake as they droned along after dark in their old pickup truck. His wife and baby were asleep, so he had to keep himself alert and awake. He didn't want to take time to pull over and nap for a bit and was frustrated that the old truck got noisy and shaky at speeds over fifty miles an hour. An added problem was that on those Wyoming highways, range cattle often spent time on the side of the road at night because there was better than average grazing at the edge of the asphalt. Grain trucks often spilled small amounts of grain as they sped along the highway, and when it rained, the grain was washed to the edge of the highway, where it grew.

So, as Bill rumbled along in his old truck, he had to keep an extra sharp lookout for cattle, which often slowly crossed the road in groups to get to the other side for better grazing. He told me that he was to the point of rubbing his whiskers, shifting positions, pressing the gas pedal with his left foot for variety, rolling down the window and flying his left hand up and down in the slip stream of air, and anything else he could do to keep his half-closed eyes from closing completely. At about that point, he sleepily thought he saw something white on the road, far ahead, at the limits of his headlights' reach. His groggy brain struggled to process it but instructed him to drive out around whatever it was. As he did so, his now more alert mind told him that it was a white fiberglass removable roof of a Corvette sports car.

Processing this as he steered back into his lane, he recalled that a while back, a white Corvette had rapidly come up the highway behind him and zoomed past at a wonderfully high rate of speed, quickly disappearing down the road. He was smitten with a pang of jealousy and momentarily wished that he and his little family were in the Corvette and its occupants were rumbling along in his old truck. It would get them home so much faster! Then he reminded himself of the commandment

"Thou shalt not covet," scolded himself briefly, and settled back into trying to stay awake and drive.

But, as he drove along, his mind continued to process things. Thoughts entered his tired mind to the effect that *a white Corvette roof, cows on the road, high-speed sports car built low to the ground, going under a cow fast would throw the poor thing up over the windshield, occupants of the Corvette possibly injured, now in trouble . . .* Slowly, it occurred to him that the Corvette might have gone off the road and wrecked. He should turn around, go back, and check the fiberglass roof for cow hair on the leading edge. He continued down the road, thinking, as he later told me, "They would have seen the cow, ducked down, and even if they had lost the windshield and roof, it is a warm night, and they could just keep on going." With that, he continued down the road. He didn't want to further delay the trip home. But he was now wide-awake.

The thought persisted. *Go back and check it out.* He wrestled back and forth with it. He thought, *Don't waste time. They are no doubt far down the road by now. Somebody else will come along and check it out.* But the thought would not leave. Finally, he stopped his old truck, turned around, and started back up the road. His wife woke up and asked what he was doing. He told her, and she helped him watch for the roof. It was still on the road, and Bill stopped his truck so the lights would shine on it. Sure enough, there was brown cow hair on the leading edge. Now wide-awake, Bill put the roof in the pickup bed, turned around, and drove slowly back along the highway. He weaved the truck back and forth, from side to side, so that the headlights would shine on the sagebrush at the sides of the road—first one side and then the other—in hopes of discovering a path of damage that would indicate if the Corvette had left the road.

Not much farther along, the headlights revealed a trail of damage angling off to the right through the brush. Bill parked off the road, grabbed a flashlight, and hurriedly followed the tracks through the brush until he came to a deep ravine. At the bottom, on the far side, lay the Corvette with its nose partially crumpled against the side of the gulch. Bill told me that he quickly slid down the side of the ravine, shined the light into the roofless car, and was startled to hear the occupant in the passenger seat say, "Bill! How did you know we were here?"

It was a good friend of his! Both passengers were seriously injured, but their lives were saved because of the prompting that "pressed" itself on Bill's mind until he obeyed it. He was able to get help for them. Only then did he realize that he had been inspired. This is often the case. If you are aware that "things that press upon your mind" are some of the common ways that inspiration comes, you can learn to be better at recognizing and acting upon them.

PEACE

Oliver Cowdery

The devil cannot counterfeit peace. (See *The Promised Messiah*, Bruce R. McConkie, Deseret Book, 1978, p. 210.) Therefore, peace is a very reliable source of inspiration and can be a rather easy form of revelation to recognize. If you try to fake it by rationalizing your sinful behavior or whatever, it won't last. If it is from God, it will remain even if you may have momentary doubts under circumstances when it is not the answer you expected. Peace comes from God and passes the test of time.

A good example of peace as a form of inspiration is found in the life of Oliver Cowdery, who became one of the Three Witnesses to the Book of Mormon. By way of background, Oliver was a young schoolteacher in the Manchester township area of upstate New York (close to Palmyra) who had contracted to teach school there during the 1828–1829 school year. Part of his pay for teaching was to rotate among the families of his students for his room and board. During this time, he heard much talk around town about Joseph and the gold plates, angelic visitations, and so forth. When his turn came to board with Joseph's parents and siblings, he found that they were reluctant to say much around him about Joseph, which fueled Oliver's curiosity. Neighbors were already ridiculing them because of Joseph and the gold plates, so they were reluctant to say much about it to Oliver. At this time, Joseph and his wife, Emma, were living on her parent's farm in Harmony, Pennsylvania, somewhat over a hundred miles from Palmyra.

Because of his curiosity, Oliver Cowdery secretly prayed one night in his heart to ask God if what he was hearing about Joseph Smith was part of the Lord's work. He told no one about his prayer. The answer he received was that of peace about Joseph's work. This peace persisted and motivated Oliver to travel to Pennsylvania to visit Joseph and Emma. He arrived April 5th and soon began serving as Joseph's scribe as the translation of the gold plates resumed. Sometime in April, Oliver received a revelation through the Prophet Joseph, in which he was reminded of the peace that had entered his soul back in Palmyra in answer to his prayer. He was thus reminded of something that no one else knew in order to strengthen his testimony about the work Joseph was doing. Peace is a powerful form of inspiration.

D&C 6:22–23

22 Verily, verily, I say unto you, if you desire a further witness, cast your mind upon the night that you cried unto me in your heart, that you might know concerning the truth of these things.

23 **Did I not speak peace to your mind concerning the matter? What greater witness can you have than from God?**

A Personal Experience

Peace, as an answer to prayer, played an important role in my life several years ago when I very much wanted to be healed of the flu. It was an occasion during my fourth year of teaching seminary in a small coal-mining town in eastern Utah. It was a Friday, and the small high school there had an away football game that afternoon. Consequently, school was to be let out at noon so those of the student body who so desired could travel to support the team. It had been a particularly busy week for me as far as extra church meetings and responsibilities were concerned, and I was looking forward to spending Friday afternoon at home. However, in the wee hours of the morning Friday, I woke up sick with the stomach flu. I hoped for it to pass quickly so I might still teach my morning classes, but it didn't. About 6:30 that morning, I called a substitute teacher and made arrangements for her to take over that day, which she willingly agreed to do.

Despite my prayers for healing as the morning drew on, my illness became worse. Finally, shortly after noon, as I lay on the front room couch, I could hear several cars passing by our house, indicating that school was out. I recognized the sounds of several modified "cool" cars belonging to some of my students as they headed to the game or wherever. For a few brief moments, I felt sorry for myself. I had spent so much of my spare time in the work of the Lord for the past several days, and He had kept me healthy when I was on His errand. But now, when I had a little time of my own, He let me get sick. I felt a tinge of irritation but quickly called myself to repentance and rolled over on the couch and got sicker.

Shortly, the thought occurred to me that I could call on a couple of elders among the men of the ward, get administered to, get well, and enjoy the afternoon and evening. But, as I thought about it more, I feared that this would be a miracle, and I would thus become a "sign seeker." I remembered a verse of scripture that says, "A wicked and adulterous generation seeketh after a sign" (Matthew 16:4). A few minutes later, I thought, *But I am not a sign seeker. I am not a wicked and adulterous generation. I would still be faithful to the Lord and the gospel if I got administered to but didn't get healed.* As I continued to contemplate my situation, I got sicker.

I soon determined to send up a "feeler prayer," so to speak, to see if it was okay to call someone to administer to me so I could be healed and have the rest of the day with good health. I said a little prayer to that effect, "ducked" in my mind in case it turned out to be an inappropriate request, rolled over, and the illness remained.

However, I felt no negative impressions from the Spirit regarding the feeler prayer. Rather, I had a mild feeling of peace. So I began mulling over in my mind who might be available to administer to me. I could think of no one who wasn't involved in the game, on shift in the coal mines, or out of town working.

Then I thought of one of my former students who had recently returned from a mission. My wife called his home. I can still hear the short conversation in my mind as she asked if he were home and his mother said, "No."

My wife asked, "Do you know when he will be home?"

"No, he is out cruising around with his friends."

His mother asked if she should have him call us when he did get home. My wife said, "No," and that was the end of that hope.

I resigned myself to my plight, but awhile later, I began thinking that the Lord knew where the returned missionary and his friends were, so why not ask Him to inspire him to come to our home? I felt peaceful about it, so I did. My faith had been strengthened by the peace that continued to prevail during my feeler prayers.

About five minutes later, there was a knock at the door. The returned missionary was there! He felt awkward and confessed that he didn't know why but had simply felt that he ought to come see "Brother Dave." Can you imagine what that did to my faith? My wife invited him in. I told him I wanted to be administered to so I could be healed. It made him a bit nervous, but he had seen another returned missionary arrive home a few minutes earlier. He called him and he came. They used their priesthood in my behalf. I was healed instantly and enjoyed the blessing of a free afternoon and evening.

Peace gave me permission to exercise faith to be healed.

CONSCIENCE

An Instant Guide

Have you ever noticed that when you decide to do something wrong, peace departs from you? That is not to say that the Holy Ghost immediately leaves you. In fact, He stays with you, initially giving you a strong and lasting feeling that you need to change plans and choose the right. But the peace leaves.

On the other hand, when you are involved in something that is sinful, and you decide to repent and switch paths to the one following the iron rod, a feeling of peace comes immediately into your heart and mind. It is revelation to you that you have made the right choice.

DREAMS AND VISIONS

Guidance from Above

Another way in which revelation and inspiration can come to us is through dreams and visions. Nephi's father, Lehi, is a great example of this type of communication to us from God.

1 Nephi 1:8

> 8 And being thus overcome with the Spirit, he was carried away in **a vision**, even that he saw the heavens open, and he thought he saw God sitting upon his throne, surrounded with numberless concourses of angels in the attitude of singing and praising their God.

Sometimes, it is hard to tell the difference between a vision and a dream. And, since both are ways in which the Lord communicates with us, it is really not necessary to try to distinguish between the two.

A Seminary Student's Dream

Some years ago, one of my seminary students had a dream that resulted in the conversion of one of her non-LDS classmates at the high school. She waited after class one day, and when the other students were gone, she told me of a dream she'd had the night before. She asked me if I thought it was from God. We briefly discussed the fact that her bishop was the only one with the authority to give her a definite answer on the matter. She said she understood that but wanted my opinion. She went on to give me a bit of background for the dream.

Every day, when it was time for seminary, one of her best friends at the high school, who was not LDS, walked with her from the school to the beginning of the seminary property where she always stopped and said goodbye, refusing to set foot on seminary property. In the course of daily conversations with my student, the girl told her that she attended seminary classes held by her church and that she had been warned that non-LDS students were not welcome in the Mormon seminary. In fact, she had been warned that three evil spirits resided in the LDS seminary building; namely, the three seminary teachers, of which I was the principal. That is why the girl obediently refused to set foot on our seminary property.

In my student's dream, she and her friend were walking as usual toward our building for her class, but in the dream, she asked her non-LDS friend if she would like to attend class with her. Startled, her friend said that she thought she was not allowed. Reassured that she would be very welcome, the friend agreed to come with her to class, which she did. Then my student woke up and the dream ended.

One of the ways to tell if a dream is from God or just a normal dream is that you can remember it clearly and the details don't become blurry upon waking or shortly thereafter. The details of the dream remained clear and impactful on her mind, so she was there, chatting with me about it.

Reminding her again that I would merely give her my opinion, I told her that if it were me, I would ask her friend if she would like to attend our seminary class with her. She asked her. She was surprised that it was permissible and excitedly and somewhat cautiously came to class the next day. She loved the class and the Holy Ghost, which she felt there. She continued attending and soon was baptized. The last time I saw her, she was married in the temple, strong in the Church, and had a beautiful family of her own.

Rescued by a Dream of "Filthy Water"

One of my institute students came to my office one day and told me of a recent dream. She had written it down and read me some of the details from the somewhat disturbing dream. She was hanging out with several of her friends beside a river that had filthy water in it. Her friends decided to play in the river. She begged them not to. They ignored her pleading and continued walking into deeper and deeper water, laughing and joking and beckoning for her to follow. Out of concern for their safety, she took on the role of rescuer and followed them out. As she continued, she felt the swift undercurrent pulling at her and stopped. Soon her friends began to fear that they were in too deep and reached for her outstretched hand but couldn't reach it. They begged her to come toward them a little farther so they could grasp her hand, but she knew that if she went out any farther, she, too, would be swept away and drowned. In agony, she turned toward the shore, and her friends were swept away and drowned.

Upon awakening from the dream, she was disturbed, but when she calmed down some, she wrote it. Now, she was in my office asking me to read it. After reading it, I asked if she had read Lehi's dream in the

Book of Mormon and Nephi's vision of it. She said yes. I asked her what she felt the message of the dream was. With tears in her eyes, she said she was sure that the people in the filthy river represented her current group of friends who were all LDS but, being away from home and in college now, they were experimenting with many things prohibited by the gospel. She viewed herself as a rescuer and also wanted friends, so she persisted in going along with them. She concluded that the message of the dream to her was that she would have to leave that group of friends or she would be swept away into forbidden paths herself. She obeyed the message and no doubt was spared much misery that would have been hers had she not been obedient. She was lonely for some time but eventually found friends who appreciated and lived the standards set by the gospel for our safety and well-being.

It is often the case that things we have read in the scriptures are used by the Holy Ghost to give us messages of warning, encouragement, and help.

VOICES

Warnings, Encouragement, and More

Voices can be audible or simply come into our mind. Often we can't tell the difference. Enos, in the Book of Mormon, is an example of this form of communication from the Lord.

> Enos 1:5, 10
>
> 5 And **there came a voice unto me**, saying: Enos, thy sins are forgiven thee, and thou shalt be blessed.
>
> 10 And while I was thus struggling in the spirit, behold, **the voice of the Lord came into my mind** again.

Mom's Life Was Spared by Obeying a Voice

My mother's life was spared when she heard a voice clearly tell her "Best if you get out." She loved going on Jeep rides in the Red Rock country of Utah and showed no fear at all when the ride involved climbing steep, seemingly impossible "roads" over rough terrain. On this particular occasion, she was riding with my brother in his highly modified Jeep and had enjoyed the ride thus far. When they came to a particularly steep and challenging obstacle, she was perfectly comfortable to ride up it with him. This part of the trail was known as "Potato Salad Hill," because, among other things, there were lots of loose rocks on the steepest part. However, she had become skilled at recognizing and obeying inspiration over the years, and now, as she approached her eighties, she again obeyed. Upon hearing the voice, she got out of the Jeep, moved off the trail a safe distance, and watched my brother attempt to climb up where few had been successful that day. Because of the difficulty of that particular obstacle, a large crowd of onlookers had gathered there, including photographers from magazines that specialized in four-wheel-drive trails and excursions.

The fans watched in fascination as my brother skillfully negotiated the steep ascent, almost to the top, and then, in horror, as the front of the Jeep reared up, pivoted over to one side, and rolled down, down, down the hill, bouncing and spilling its contents through the roll cage. My brother was securely belted in as the Jeep rolled several times. It was all caught on video by many cameras. Sequence photos of it appeared in a popular off-road magazine. The passenger side that Mom had been riding in took the brunt of the damage. We have no doubt that she would have been killed had she chosen to ignore the clear voice. In discussing it with us later, she suggested that the reason the voice said, "Best if you get out," rather than "Get out!" was that, at her age, and with Dad having passed away already, it would not have been a tragedy for her to die doing what she loved to do and rejoin her husband in paradise. In fact, she had told us many times that she wanted to die with her "boots on." However, it would have been extremely hard on my brother. So, it was "best" that she "get out."

3

HOW DO I KNOW IF I HAVE A TESTIMONY?

Some youth of the Church wonder if they have a testimony. When this is the case, it is often because they have not learned to recognize warm feelings and impressions that come from the Spirit during daily life, including when we are reading our scriptures.

She Was Expecting Something Spectacular and Was Missing the "Still, Small Voice"

A friend of mine told me that his daughter, who was a junior in high school, decided she did not have a testimony despite being faithful and active in the Church and seminary. It had been a busy day for my friend, who was serving as a bishop at the time. When he arrived home from work, he had just enough time to clean up for his evening meetings, get a quick bite to eat, and dash to the church. On his way from the garage through the kitchen to his bedroom, he noticed that his daughter was at the sink doing dishes and crying. As he hurried on through the kitchen, he thought, *If I were doing dishes, I'd be crying too!* Just before he exited the kitchen, his better senses as a father took over.

He stopped and asked his daughter why she was crying. She replied through sobs, "I don't have a testimony!"

Startled, he blurted out, "What do you mean? I thought you said you have been faithfully reading your chapter a day from the scriptures."

She replied, "I have, for 634 days in a row."

He followed by asking if she hadn't felt the Spirit at least sometimes during her reading. She responded that she had thought so, but now she realized that she didn't really have a testimony.

Coming back into the kitchen, he stepped closer to her and tenderly asked why she suddenly felt that way.

She replied that in seminary that day, they had discussed how testimonies came to Alma the Younger and the four rebellious sons of Mosiah, who were stopped by an angel; to Saul (who was renamed "Paul"), when the Savior appeared to him as he traveled the road to Damascus to persecute Christians; and to King Lamoni, who saw the Savior during the time his body lay unconscious.

She told her father that she'd never had even close to such spectacular manifestations from God, so she obviously did not have a testimony.

Wisely and tenderly, he told her that if we expect the spectacular, we can easily miss the quiet whisperings of the Spirit to our mind and heart.

They went on to discuss Alma 32, which is about planting the seed of the gospel and carefully observing it "begin to swell within" you. Paying attention as "you feel these swelling motions" as "it beginneth to enlarge" your soul and "beginneth to enlighten" your understanding. And, ultimately, as "it beginneth to be delicious" unto you. As they chatted, she recalled having had many such feelings as she read the scriptures and attended church, seminary, and family home evenings. She'd also experienced those feelings during girls' camp testimony meetings. She finally realized that she did have a testimony. She just hadn't recognized it for what it was.

Spectacular manifestations from heaven can and do come on special occasions, but they are usually few and far between. The real substance of testimony comes as described in Alma 32:27–43, gradually, reliably, and consistently. The Spirit warms the heart and brings peace to the soul. Those who learn to recognize these feelings come to understand that they are having numerous testimony building experiences daily.

4

THE POWER OF ONE

Remember, you are only one, but you are one! You have great power to help others as they strive to keep the standards of the gospel. By using your agency righteously, you have the "power of one" to influence others for good. As you know, peer pressure is difficult for many to resist, and you never know when your example in choosing the right will be the factor that frees another from the tentacles of temptation.

They All Prepared to Light Up Their Cigarettes

An acquaintance of mine told of an experience he had when he was about sixteen and an Aaronic Priesthood holder. He and other members of his priest's quorum were hanging out together one summer's day. They were a bit bored. Then one of them came up with an idea. "Let's all eight of us pile into my dad's car, go up the canyon, park, roll up the windows, and each light up a cigarette and smoke until we see who passes out first." They all agreed, and soon they were at their destination. My friend did not want to do it for many reasons, including that it would be breaking the Word of Wisdom, but he figured that the other guys wanted to do it, and he didn't have the courage to say no.

The driver pulled out a pack of cigarettes and a lighter. The pack was passed around, and each young man in the front bench seat of the big sedan took a cigarette. Then the pack of cigarettes was passed to the back seat passengers. My friend was second to last and sweating in agony as his turn approached. Imagine his relief when the friend to his right hesitated and said, "Guys, I don't want to do it." Immediately, the others chimed in and agreed. Somewhat subdued, they all put their cigarettes back into the pack and handed it to the owner. My friend told us of his tremendous relief and also his embarrassment that he had not had the courage himself to refuse. But his determination was greatly strengthened to be the one to stand for the right from that point on in his life.

The Savior asked us to use our own "power of one" to help Him in His work.

> Matthew 5:16
>
> 16 **Let your light so shine before men, that they may see your good works**, and glorify your Father which is in heaven.

The Altar Boy Who Kept Verbally Attacking My Seminary Students

As a seminary teacher in the coal mining country of eastern Utah, I frequently heard of a Catholic altar boy attending the high school. He was a senior who seemed to take delight in verbally tearing down the beliefs of our seminary students. He would spot them carrying their LDS scriptures in the halls of the school and confront them, using his superior knowledge of the Bible to "bash" with them. Often, my students would come to seminary looking somewhat battered. I could see a certain look in their eyes and would ask them if the altar boy had gotten hold of them. The answer was usually yes.

The school year was well along, and I had not yet met this senior who was giving many of my students such a rough time about our Church, but one day, that all changed. After class, one of the girls lingered and asked me if I would be willing to talk with the altar boy. She was cute and had become friends with him, and he'd asked if it might be possible for him to talk with one of the LDS seminary teachers. She told him she would find out. She did, and it was agreed that they would come to the seminary after school that day and meet with me in my office at 4:00 p.m. As she left the room, I thought, *So, he's tired of devouring small fish and wants to try his teeth on a big one (me) at the LDS seminary*. I was sort of joking with myself, but there was an element of reality in what I was thinking.

Four o'clock came, and I heard the back door of the seminary open, followed by heavy footsteps alongside light footsteps. Down the hall, they came to my office. My door was open, and as I stood to welcome them, I sensed that he was excited about the potential of doing battle with me. I invited them to sit down and asked him if it would be okay if we had a word of prayer. He agreed, and I asked the girl if she would say it. During the afternoon, since her class, I had done some praying and considerable thinking about what approach to use with him. I decided to use a missionary discussion I taught on my mission. However, during the prayer, the thought came strongly into my mind to ask him if he was aware that we have a Mother in Heaven. For a split second I resisted, thinking that this topic was the last one we should discuss on a first meeting. But I quickly yielded to what I recognized as a "sudden thought" of inspiration.

When the prayer was over, he leaned forward somewhat, as if preparing for dinner, and I said, "Before we start, are you aware that we have a Mother in Heaven?"

In an instant, it was as if all of his carefully prepared anti-LDS ammunition fell from his mind onto the floor of my office. His head jerked back, he paled a little, and with a completely changed look on his face, he sincerely said, "I've always wondered about that. I've always felt that we do, but I have not been able to ask or discuss it with anyone without being scolded or warned not to even think such heresy. Do we?" The answer was yes, but we really don't know any more. We even have an LDS Hymn, "O My Father," which includes a verse that says, "Truth is reason, truth eternal, tells me I have a mother there." He loved it!

We went on to discuss the plan of salvation and answer many of his questions. He was completely humble and interested. Soon, the missionaries became involved, and before long, he was baptized and confirmed. He went on to serve a full-time mission for the Church and marry in the temple. Some years later, he called and told me that he was serving in a stake presidency. The next call for him was to serve as a mission president.

My sweet and courageous student, a senior herself, clearly exemplified the "power of one" as she invited her non-LDS, rather antagonistic friend to come to the seminary and ask about our beliefs. Of course, it helped that she was cute!

They Ran the Seminary Teacher Out of Town

Another example of the "power of one" is found in my first year of teaching seminary. I was assigned to a small released-time seminary in Utah's coal country as the only teacher. I was unaware that the previous seminary teacher had been, in effect, run out of town by the mean and unruly behaviors of the students. Because of their dislike for that teacher and their mean pranks directed toward him and his little family, the bishops of the two wards in the area had requested to the Church Educational System administrators that he be transferred to another seminary to teach. There was a high degree of curiosity on the part of the students and parents as to who the next teacher would be.

At the time of my assignment to teach in that community for the coming fall, I was living with my wife and two small children in a tiny rented house in Pinedale, Wyoming, where, for a summer job, I was working as a lumberjack on the East Rim of the Hoback River, about ninety miles east of Jackson. Upon getting the appointment, my wife and I made a quick trip to the location of my new teaching assignment, where the bishops treated us kindly and helped us find a home to rent. Near the end of August, we arrived in town pulling a U-Haul trailer and moved in.

On our second night in town, after dark, there was a rather loud and heavy knock on our door. We opened it and saw a group of five young men standing there. One, a big fellow who was obviously the spokesman, asked in a loud, gruff voice, "Are you the new seminary teacher?" I said yes, and with no further conversation with us, he turned to the rest of them and said, "It's him. Let's go in." We moved out of the way, they came in, sat down, and spent the next hour talking among themselves, completely ignoring us, other than accepting some popcorn my wife had popped.

After about an hour, the big one (I'll call him Clint, which is not his real name) turned and looked to where we were standing and said, "Guys, I think we're leaving them out." Then, to us, he said, "Sit down."

We did. We listened with interest as they continued to talk among themselves, laughing and recalling a number of their exploits, including a time when Clint broke one of his front teeth partway off.

They'd been on a wrestling team trip to another town, and part of their entertainment in the local motel was seeing if they could successfully crash through the wall into the room where other members of the team were staying. Of course, they had to hit the wall in between two-by-four studs in order to make it. Clint missed and broke a front tooth part way off against a stud. They all laughed at this as he retold it in our living room. Finally, they started including us in the conversation, and I related some of my experiences lumberjacking. After a while, he looked at us and said, "Hey guys, it's getting late. We better go so Brother and Sister Ridges can go to bed." They went. We looked at each other and said, "Wow, what have we gotten ourselves into?" But we were grinning.

A few days later, I went with a few of the students, including Clint, and scouted out a location along a stream where we could have a seminary opening social picnic. It was a warm afternoon, and the kids were playing and throwing each other into the river. I snuck up behind Clint when he was off balance in the water and tipped all 265 pounds of him soundly into the river. I figured as big as he was, I could easily outrun him through the sagebrush. He was fast! Just as he caught up to me and was directly behind me, I tripped over some sagebrush. I tried to cushion my fall with my arms and my left elbow pressed against my left side. He fell on top of me, and we heard a distinct cracking sound from one of my ribs. He helped me up, apologizing profusely, and we walked back to the picnic site. As we began gathering things up to go home, I sneezed, and everyone heard a loud cracking sound. I was indeed hurting but having a hard time not laughing. They all rallied around me, especially Clint, and from that time on, he was my good friend and self-appointed bodyguard. The cracked rib, later treated by a doctor, was probably the best thing that could have happened to help me get established on good terms with the seminary students there.

As the time for school approached, at least two teachers from the high school came at separate times to the seminary to visit with me. Each of them, after introducing themselves and getting acquainted, asked me to be sure to pass Clint, who was a senior. At that time, schools in Utah were allowed to give credit toward high school graduation to seminary students who were taking Church history classes in seminary, since it included the history of settling Utah by the pioneers. They told me that he was just plain dumb, that he had low IQ scores, and they just wanted him to graduate so they could be done with him. They assured me that there was consensus among all of his teachers, and they had all agreed to give him a passing grade, even if it was a D-, in order to graduate him. I told them I would see what I could do and thanked them for coming to visit.

Soon, school started. One evening at about 7:30, I was tending our children while my wife was at a Young Women's meeting at the church. There was a familiar, heavy knock on the door. I opened it, and there stood Clint, with about fourteen other students, some in seminary, and some not. They had brought several chess sets and asked if I would mind if they played chess for a while at our home. I was tickled to have them come and invited them in. They spread out all over the carpet, and when my wife, Janette, came home, fourteen chess games were going! I told them I didn't really remember how to play chess, which was true, and that I would just watch.

A few days later, during Clint's seminary class, out of the blue, he challenged me to a chess match in front of the class. I reminded him that I didn't remember much about how to play, and he assured me that he would teach me. I thought it interesting that a supposedly "dumb" kid was going to play chess in front of everybody, along with trying to teach me how, which takes a good amount of intelligence. At that point, the class was more interested in watching a chess match between Clint and Brother Dave (that's what they called me, and they called my wife "Sister Dave") than having the regular lesson. So, I said, "Why not?" and we set up for the game.

He reminded me of the basic chess moves. (I remembered them vaguely because I had played a few games with my brother some years back.) Then he proceeded to beat me five times in a row with just a few moves! Ouch! The class loved it, as did he. I thought, *For a supposedly dumb kid, he sure is smart!*

As the year progressed, we were studying Doctrine and Covenants and Church history. We were dealing with Joseph Smith and the Restoration. I noticed that Clint was quick to participate in class discussions and knew answers to almost all of my review questions about things we had already discussed. In fact, he became my best ally in class. If students were talking to each other during class, he would call them out and say, "Hey! Stop talking. Brother Dave is teaching." And he meant it. They would stop talking. He was a big guy!

The day came when I told them that the next day, we would have a quiz on what we had discussed so far. I told them that in class today, I would ask them questions and help with answers. Clint knew virtually all the answers. I finally had to grin at him and ask him to give others a chance. Once in a while, when nobody could come up with the answer, he would raise his hand and give it. I still remember one of his answers. The question was "Where did Joseph and Emma get married?" Nobody knew the answer. He slowly raised his hand and said, "I know. They got married in South Bainbridge, New York, on January 18, 1827. They had to elope because her dad didn't want her marrying a gold-diggin' prophet guy who was embarrassing the family. And Emma was older than Joseph." Wow!

The next day in class, I asked the students to move everything off their desks onto the floor, except a pen or pencil. Then I handed out copies of the quiz to each one. It was quiet as they went to work. I slowly made my way around the room and along between the desks. When I got to Clint, I noticed that he had not written anything on his quiz. He looked up at me a bit embarrassed. I quietly knelt by his desk, pointed to a question on the quiz that asked when the First Vision was, and whispered to him, "Clint, you know when the First Vision was."

He whispered back, "I know, it was spring 1820."

I pointed to the appropriate space on his paper and said, "Right. Write it here."

His face flushed, and he said, "How do you spell "spring?"

Immediately, it dawned on me! Clint couldn't read! He was highly intelligent, but in his particular school setting all his life, he had been considered intellectually slow, and no one had taken the time to figure out what he needed.

I quietly gave him the quiz orally, whispering the test questions to him and listening to his whispered answers. He got 100%. He was smart! I gave him an A+. He was very happy. His self-image changed dramatically. I gave him every test that way for the rest of the year. His entire self-image as a person and as a member of the Church changed completely. He learned that he was highly capable, and so did others. It turned out that he had dyslexia. That's when a word such as "was" appears as "saw" to the one with dyslexia. It makes reading difficult unless specific help is received.

As mentioned above, Clint's image of himself changed dramatically. Feeling that he was not "dumb," but rather intelligent and highly capable, he determined to serve a mission. During his mission, he learned how to read, primarily using the Book of Mormon. Upon his return, he determined to pursue a career that required reading and speaking proficiency.

In this case, the Lord used me to be the one who made a difference initially for Clint. When I am privileged to help do the Lord's work, I always try to offer up a prayer of gratitude to Heavenly Father, giving Him the credit and the glory, but expressing my thanks for the privilege of being on the team.

The Institute Student Who Glared Defiantly at Me

It was about two weeks into a new semester at the Orem Institute of Religion where I was teaching. One day, about ten minutes into a Book of Mormon class, a young man quietly opened the classroom door and sat down in an empty desk on the front row, close to the door. I paused the lesson, smiled at him, and welcomed him to class. He said nothing in return, slouched down in the desk, and glared at me for the rest of the class. I noticed his lack of response to what was going on in the class and determined to make sure I approached him after class to get acquainted. But immediately after the closing prayer, other students caught me with additional questions and comments, and despite my best efforts, he slipped out before I could get to him.

As I went back to my office after class, I mused to myself that I would likely never see him again and was sorry that I had missed the chance to at least chat with him. I was surprised to see him again in the next class, in the same desk, and with the same doubtful, glowering look toward me throughout the class. Again, I determined to catch him right after class. Again, I missed. The same scenario played out for two or three more classes. Then, one day at the end of class, he lingered and asked if he could visit with me in my office. The answer was yes. I was glad he had asked.

Seated in my office, he told me the story behind his coming into that institute class. He was a returned missionary, back from his mission about three years. He lived in the southern states and had eventually gone inactive from the Church over the course of several months after returning. His life was in a downward spiral, and he felt lost and unfulfilled. He tried some college courses in the area where he lived but found little satisfaction. Many of his friends were attending school in Utah but, as he told me, coming to Utah was the last thing he wanted to do, especially since he was trying to avoid the Church. In a strange twist of events, which at the time of our conversation he still could not explain completely, he ended up in Utah at what is now Utah Valley University. This was his second semester.

He explained that he had carefully avoided any contact with the Church here but had become curious about a large building on campus. (It really wasn't on campus, because it was our institute of religion building, on Church-owned property, right next to campus. But he didn't know that, and we didn't yet have our name on the building.) It was the same architectural style as the other buildings on campus, and, over time, he began wondering why he never had classes in that building.

He continued his story, telling me that one day, his curiosity got the best of him, and, with a little time on his hands, he approached the main entrance to our building from campus and looked through the double glass doors, trying to see what was in the lobby. He couldn't see much, so he opened the first door and stepped into the space between the first and second set of doors. He said that the strong, pleasant Spirit he felt caught him off guard. He stopped, looked around, and said, "No way! What is this?" He thought he must be imagining that vaguely familiar feeling from the past, so he turned around and exited the building. He then stopped, turned around, and decided to try it again. He entered and again felt the overwhelming pleasantness of the Spirit. It was not his imagination.

Puzzled but curious, he stepped through the next set of glass doors into the lobby and lounge, which served as the front office, as well as a place for students to mingle between classes. He saw students sitting on couches, playing ping-pong, chatting and visiting, studying, relaxing, and enjoying hanging out. As he stood just inside the doors, one of our institute student council members noticed him and the puzzled look on his face. She immediately approached him and welcomed him to institute. She asked if he would like her to show him around. He said yes. Soon, she asked if he had signed up for a class yet. He said no. So, she showed him a class schedule and invited him to sign up for one. He told me that at that point he had mixed feelings. He was determined to avoid contact with the Church, but this felt so good! Soon he yielded to the girl's pleasant persuasion and that of the Holy Ghost and signed up for a class that fit into his schedule. The class happened to be one I was teaching.

As he finished his story in my office, he explained his rather intense, seemingly unpleasant behavior toward me when he first attended my class. He said that after he signed up for the class, it dawned on him what he had done, and he decided to leave and never come back. It was a tug of war between that determination and the fresh memory of the pleasant feelings that warmed his somewhat dried up soul during his unplanned visit. Not only was the girl pleasant and friendly, but he also noticed numerous other students in the building who radiated the same warmth and welcome. So, he came to class to try it out. He was intense as he tried to sort out whether the Spirit was genuine or if it was just his imagination. It was real.

Just one institute student who had responded to the Spirit's prompting to welcome a soul who had strayed made all the difference. The young man found out which ward he was in, became acquainted with the bishop, and it changed his entire direction in life. Again, we see the "power of one." It is doubtful that the student council member had any idea of the miracle of rescue that she started in motion that day.

Joseph in Egypt Was a Prime Example of the "Power of One"

Joseph was the one whose father, Jacob, had given him a coat of many colors. He was seventeen years old when his jealous older brothers sold him into Egyptian slavery. Among other things, the brothers strongly disliked Joseph because of two prophetic dreams he'd had that foretold how his brothers and parents would someday bow down to him. You can read about these in Genesis 37:2–10. Imagine the drastic change in Joseph's prospects for the future that came when he was sold into slavery! Finding himself in Egypt as a slave, completely separated from his family, with terribly dismal prospects for his future, he could have given up all hope. But he didn't.

In Egypt, Potiphar, a high-ranking official in Pharaoh's court (Genesis 39:1) purchased him. Joseph remained true to his commitments to God and did his best in everything required of him in Potiphar's house. Consequently, the Lord blessed him, and he soon was made overseer of Potiphar's entire household. Over time, Potiphar's wife became obsessed with this handsome Hebrew slave, Joseph, and did all she could to entice him to become involved with her in sexual immorality. He refused, saying, "How then can I do this great wickedness, and sin against God?" (Genesis 39:9).

Undeterred, she persisted in her attempts to tempt Joseph, day after day. Finally, in desperation, one day when she was alone with him in the house, she grabbed him by his clothing, pleading with him to satisfy her desires. Joseph tore loose from her, leaving a piece of his clothing in her hands. He "fled and got him out" (Genesis 39:12). Furious and rejected, she screamed for help, falsely accused Joseph, and got him thrown into a dungeon reserved for the king's prisoners. Imagine how Joseph felt! He had chosen the right, and look at the consequences! But he had a clear conscience before God, which is priceless.

Briefly, as recorded in Genesis 39–41, Joseph spent the next several years in prison, but the Lord blessed him, and conditions improved for him. His lifestyle, even in prison, enabled the Lord to bless him richly.

Over time, two of the king's servants, the chief butler and the chief baker, got into trouble with the king and were cast into prison, and Joseph was put in charge of taking care of them (Genesis 40:1–4). Both men had dreams that foretold their future, and Joseph, with inspiration from God, interpreted them. According to the inspired interpretation of the butler's dream, he was to be released from prison in three days and reinstated in the service of the king. He was. Joseph asked the butler to speak a good word to the king for him when he was restored to his former position, but he forgot.

When the baker heard the encouraging interpretation by Joseph of the butler's dream, he asked him to interpret his. Joseph's interpretation was that in three days, the baker would be executed by the king's order. He was.

The initial groundwork was now laid for Joseph to be in a position to exercise the "power of one" for the Egyptian people, as well as for his father's family. The next step would require two more years (Genesis 41:1). At that point, Pharaoh had two troubling dreams; one in which he saw seven fat, healthy cows appear first, and then seven skinny cattle came and ate the seven fat ones. In the next dream, he first saw seven healthy, plump heads of grain growing on a single stalk, followed by seven poorly developed heads of grain, blasted by the hot, dry, east wind, which ate the healthy heads of grain. Disturbed by these dreams, he called for his wise men, told them the dreams, and asked them for an interpretation. They couldn't come up with one. Under these pressing circumstances, the butler remembered that Joseph had successfully interpreted his dream and that of the baker.

He told Pharaoh, and Pharaoh summoned Joseph from the prison. He described his dreams to Joseph. Joseph told him that he could not interpret dreams, but his God could. The interpretation was that Egypt would have seven years of plenty, followed by seven years of poor crops that would lead to famine. At the end of interpreting the Pharaoh's dreams, Joseph counseled the king to select a wise man and appoint him to be in charge of a large organization assigned to collect and store one fifth of the crops during each of the good years in order to prepare the land for the famine that would follow. After consulting with his leading men, Pharaoh appointed Joseph to be second in command over all of Egypt and to supervise the food storage program.

Joseph was now in a position to exercise the "power of one" to save the Egyptians from famine. He would likewise save his own father's family from starvation when they came to Egypt to buy supplies (Genesis 42–46).

By the way, Joseph was thirty years old when he was made second in command in Egypt (Genesis 41:46). He was seventeen years old (Genesis 37:2) when he was sold into slavery. Thus, he spent about thirteen years living his religion against all odds, most of that time in prison, before his "power of one" came into full play to save many.

I Forgave Him

During a rather busy part of my career, I was teaching a fairly large adult religion class in my community on Wednesday evenings after school where I was teaching at the local high school seminary. In the middle of that particular school year, the high school administration had requested that the seminary teachers join them in their campaign to cut down on the number of students coming late to their classes. We agreed and decided that, where necessary, we would involve parents in helping us solve the problem. Also, the high school told us that if we had students who would not shape up in this matter, we could send them back to the school, and their released-time privileges would be revoked. Our students were good at responding to our efforts, so the problem was under control.

However, I had a senior in my 1:00 p.m. class who persisted in coming about ten minutes late to class. I chatted with him, and he promised to do better. He did—for a few days—and then the pattern of coming late continued. I asked him again to come on time. He again promised to do better. He did—for a few days. Finally, I warned him that if he came late again, I would call his parents. The look on his face told me that he didn't believe me. It was almost an "I dare you," challenging look. The next day, a Tuesday, he came late yet again, so I called his parents. They were good about it and assured me they would take care of it.

On Wednesday, he was almost on time to class—just barely twenty to thirty seconds late. I had left my normal greeting position at the door and was at the front of the class, ready to begin teaching. As he came into class, our eyes met. I raised my eyebrows at him but grinned. His face flushed, and he had what I later came to see as a bit of a satisfied grin as he quickly took his seat. I let it go and continued with class.

After school, I finished my normal work hours preparing lessons and remained in my office to prepare for my adult religion class at 7:00 that evening. It took longer than expected, so at about 6:25, I quickly gathered up my teaching materials and hurried out to my car in the parking lot. I just barely had time to hurry home, grab a quick bite to eat—which my wife had ready for me—and still make it to my evening class on time. I hurried across the parking lot only to see that the right rear tire on my car was flat. I glanced quickly at my watch and thought, *I can still make it. I'll just put the spare tire on in the fastest time ever and still be all right.* As I quickly put my books in the car, I noticed that the right front tire was also completely flat! Ouch! What bad luck! I again looked at my watch. Panic!

I quickly decided that since it was only about a mile and a half to the stake center where I taught the evening class, I could use the foot pump in my trunk to pump just enough air into each tire to get me to class on time. If the leaks were not too bad, it would not damage the tires, and I could finish the repair job after class. I grabbed the pump and removed the valve cap from the rear tire in order to screw the hose onto the valve stem. As I unscrewed the cap, my eye caught a tiny piece of gravel as it dropped from inside the cap to the asphalt.

What's this doing inside the cap? How in the world did it get there?

A light in my mind suddenly went on. I stepped to the flat front tire and carefully unscrewed the valve cap. Sure enough, another tiny piece of gravel fell out.

Ingenious! I couldn't help grinning a bit as anger and frustration tried to crowd quickly into my mind. I thought of the unexplained slight grin on my student's face earlier that afternoon as he came to class. Everything came together.

Mad at me for calling his parents, he must have hurried over to the seminary parking lot and ducked down on the far side of my car where nobody would see him. He picked out a tiny piece of gravel on the asphalt, carefully put it inside my valve cap, and screwed it on far enough to make contact with the valve, which caused an almost silent stream of air to escape from the tire. He did the same to the front tire and then hurried to class.

I quickly pumped just enough air into each tire to lift the rim about an inch off the ground and drove to our home where I grabbed a few mouthfuls of food. I took our other car to class, arriving with a couple of minutes to spare.

The next day, I was curious to see if my antagonist would show up to class. I'd thought it over the night before and decided to forgive him. I'd made it a practice to shake hands with each student as they came to class, calling them by name and thanking them for coming. Sure enough, there he was, several students back in the line, and definitely on time. I noticed the embarrassed and apprehensive look on his face as he got closer. As I grasped his hand firmly, I looked him straight in the eye and whispered, "That was ingenious! I had never thought of that. And, by the way, I forgive you. Welcome to class."

His head visibly rocked back a bit. He looked startled and relieved. He took his seat. No more was said about it.

He was not tardy even once for the rest of the year. He was rather quiet in class but was pleasant and sometimes participated. We often smiled at each other as if we shared some kind of secret between us. The school year ended. He graduated from high school, married his girlfriend in a civil marriage, and moved to another state.

Three years later, I was writing curriculum materials for the Seminaries and Institutes of Religion at the Church Office Building in Salt Lake City. One day I received a letter addressed to me that had somehow found its way to me via seminary headquarters. It was from the student who had flattened my tires. In it, he thanked me for forgiving him that day. He said that my forgiving him had "haunted" (his own word) him every day after that. It was a good haunting, he said. He and his wife had had a little girl born to them, and they loved her very much. He told me in the letter that the more he thought about what it meant to him that I forgave him, the more he thought that the Church must be true if it taught to forgive like that. Gradually, he and his wife determined to get their lives in order and take their little girl to the temple to be sealed as a family. He told me that the date of their sealing was, at the time of his writing, just two weeks away. They couldn't wait! My heart thrilled as I thanked Heavenly Father—giving Him the credit—for the privilege of being on His team.

Sometimes your "power of one" can be effective in a relatively quiet and small field of play, such as when you sincerely forgive someone for something they did that hurt you or caused you difficulty. It is pleasantly surprising how much your willingness to forgive can bless such a person's life.

5

THE POWER OF THE SCRIPTURES

When you read the scriptures regularly, it gives the Holy Ghost a lot more ways to inspire and help you. For example, He can confirm a difficult course of action you are considering by recalling to your mind a similar experience in the scriptures that you have read in the past.

A Daughter's Dilemma

From the time she was little, one of our daughters spent a lot of time playing with friends in our neighborhood. They were inseparable all through elementary school and on into their mid-teens and high school. Along the way, especially as they got their driver's licenses and became more mobile, many of them quit going to church and started onto forbidden paths.

This was of great concern to us as well as our daughter, who continued her own faithful activity in the Church. By personality, she is a rescuer. She tried to talk them out of what they were doing, but it didn't work. As they got in deeper and deeper, she was often their designated driver when they left parties where alcohol and drugs were involved. She felt she was strong enough not to let the bad videos they watched and the often coarse and vulgar environment damage her spiritually, but she soon realized that it was having its effect on her. Often their parties were on Saturday night. Our daughter would hang her Levi jacket and other items of clothing outside on our deck when she got home so they would air out and not stink up her Sunday clothes in her closet.

As things went from bad to worse, she talked to us and shared her concerns. The peer pressure was high. Finally, she asked us to help her turn down invitations to attend parties she knew would be extra bad. The deal was this: When certain friends called to invite her to come with them, she would say, "Hold on. Let me ask my parents." Then she would look at whichever one of us was around and ask if she could go, shaking her head, indicating not to give permission. She would wait a few seconds and then shout with an angry voice, "Why not?" Sometimes followed up by "You never let me do anything!" or whatever. Sometimes we had a hard time keeping a straight face, and she had a rough time not giving it away by laughing. It worked.

Still, it was hard on her, because she feared for her friends, especially if she was not there to try to rescue them. It got worse and worse, and one day her mother gave her this advice: "It's not just about you. You must protect the mother of your children."

This advice had a profound effect on our daughter. It settled deep into her soul and provided much strength. She knew she wanted to be a mother and raise children in a righteous home with the standards of the gospel around them. That perspective led her to decide to pull away from her life-long friends and go it alone. It was most difficult and brought many tears.

Still struggling, one evening she asked if she could chat with me. I was glad to talk. She poured out her heart, especially about what might happen to her friends if nobody was there to pull them in the right direction, or at the very least, to drive them home when they shouldn't drive themselves.

As we talked, the thought came into my mind to ask if she had read the Book of Mormon. The answer was "Yes, many times." I asked if she remembered that Nephi had tried many times to rescue his wayward brothers and others of his group from dangerous and forbidden paths, but, ultimately, it did not work. A light of relief came on in her face. As the relief spread, she said, in effect, that she had forgotten about that. I suggested that we read it together. We did.

> 2 Nephi 5:5
>
> 5 And it came to pass that **the Lord did warn me, that I, Nephi, should depart from them and flee** into the wilderness, and all those who would go with me.

As she read this out loud, great relief washed over her face. She looked up at me and said, "Then, it is okay for me to leave them, right?" The answer, from me, the Book of Mormon, and the Holy Ghost, was a peaceful and strong "Yes."

She stopped hanging out with them and was lonely for several months. But she was determined and, reinforced by Nephi, succeeded in doing the right thing. She served a mission, married in the temple, is raising a family in the Church, and has graduated from a university. Her dreams and hopes of being a mother with a righteous home and family are now being wonderfully fulfilled.

6

THE PLAN OF SALVATION

A Primer for Prospective Missionaries

It helps tremendously if prospective missionaries have a good, basic understanding of the Father's plan of salvation as they enter the MTC. It gives them more confidence personally and is a great blessing as they help others understand the "big picture" of the gospel throughout their missions.

In the Book of Mormon, God's plan for us is called the "plan of salvation" (Alma 42:5), also known as "the great plan of happiness" (Alma 42:8). A good, basic understanding of who we are, where we came from, why we are here, what our potential is, and the essential and wonderful role of the Atonement of Jesus Christ can serve strongly as a "Liahona" to guide us through life. Also, the Holy Ghost can effectively use our understanding of our Father's plan to prompt us to do right. In other words, knowing the "whys" behind His inspiration to choose the right can greatly strengthen us when we are standing at the difficult crossroads of life.

With this in mind, I will be your teacher for a few minutes, as if you were in one of my seminary or institute classes. I will ask you some questions about the plan of salvation, by way of a quiz, so you can get a general idea of how good your basic knowledge of the Father's plan is. I have used this quiz and the resulting discussion with my students hundreds of times over many years. It is a true-false quiz, and I will give you the answers following the quiz. Take the quiz any way you want—for example, look through the questions until you see one you are not sure about and check the answer key in this book for the answer. Or, you may wish to take the entire quiz first and then check the answer key to see how you did.

You may wish to take the quiz along with some friends and then discuss your answers together before checking to see how you did. You are welcome to use your scriptures for help in answering the questions while taking the quiz. After you take the quiz and check your answers, you might consider making notes in your own scriptures alongside the scriptural references used in the answer key. After you have finished the quiz and checked your answers, I will take you through a brief overview of the plan of salvation using many of the questions my students have asked.

TRUE FALSE QUIZ: PLAN OF SALVATION

1. T F Most churches don't teach about premortal life.
2. T F As spirits in premortality, we were basically real people without physical bodies.
3. T F You first came into existence when you became a spirit child of Heavenly Parents.
4. T F You have always existed as intelligence and never did "come into existence."
5. T F Referring back to our premortality, our Heavenly Parents there had resurrected, celestial bodies of flesh and bone.
6. T F Resurrected bodies produce spirit offspring.
7. T F You were born as a spirit child to our Heavenly Parents.
8. T F Your spirit has always existed.
9. T F Spirit is actually a type of matter.
10. T F Spirit bodies have the same body parts that earthly physical bodies have.
11. T F Satan was the next oldest to Christ in the premortal life.

12. T F We all developed equally in the premortal life, because we were all in the direct presence of God.

13. T F During the War in Heaven, some people "sat on the fence"; that is to say, they couldn't decide whose side to be on.

14. T F Many people were killed in the War in Heaven.

15. T F Some faithful people in premortal life actually helped with the creation of the earth.

16. T F Satan and the one third who followed him were cast down to earth and are still here today tempting us.

17. T F Satan and the spirits who followed him are allowed not only to tempt us here on earth, but also to tempt people who have died and gone to the postmortal spirit world.

18. T F We have not yet been told where the postmortal spirit world is.

19. T F The spirit world is divided into two main categories, paradise and prison.

20. T F Only baptized, faithful members of the Church are allowed to enter paradise.

21. T F Wicked people who have died and entered the prison portion of the spirit world will then know that life continues after death and will want our missionaries there to preach the gospel to them immediately.

22. T F The veil prevents us from remembering our premortal life.

23. T F There were male spirits and female spirits in the premortal life.

24. T F When babies are born here on earth, they have full-grown spirits in them.

25. T F On rare occasions when a child who has died is permitted to appear to someone to provide comfort or whatever, he or she can appear as a child, a full-grown spirit, or whatever age is appropriate for the occasion.

26. T F Without this earth life, we could never be exalted.

27. T F After final judgment day, everyone but exalted people will be single.

28. T F In the next life, only those who attain celestial exaltation will have use of the powers of procreation and live in the family unit.

29. T F Those who achieve exaltation will create and people worlds of their own.

30. T F Because exaltation is extremely difficult to attain, few will actually get it.

31. T F Christ will wear red when He comes, representing His blood that was shed for the righteous.

32. T F There will be no significant differences between the resurrected bodies of celestial people and those of terrestrial and telestial people, because their bodies will all be perfect.

33. T F No telestial people have been resurrected yet.

34. T F We don't know how long people will live during the Millennium.

35. T F There will be no wicked people during the Millennium.

36. T F Satan will be around, trying to tempt people during the Millennium, but nobody will listen to him.

37. T F People living during the Millennium will still be mortal.

38. T F Babies who died before the age of accountability and people born during the Millennium will be tested when Satan is let loose at the end of the Millennium.

39. T F Those of us who become gods will use the same plan of salvation for our own spirit children that is being used for us.

ANSWER KEY FOR TRUE FALSE QUIZ: PLAN OF SALVATION

1. ? Jeremiah 1:5 teaches premortal life, but few, if any, Christian churches teach it or seem to believe in it as doctrine.

Therefore, you could have answered "true." However, if you were thinking in terms of non-Christian religions, many of them believe in a life or lives before this one. Therefore, you could have answered "false."

2. T See Abraham 3:18–24. Too many people don't realize that we were real, thinking, acting individuals there, as spirit sons and daughters of God.

3. F "There is something called intelligence which has always existed. It is the real eternal part of man, which was not created or made" (Joseph Fielding Smith, *The Progress of Man,* p. 10; see also D&C 93:29).

   Joseph Smith said, "The intelligence of spirits had no beginning" (*History of the Church*, vol. 6, p. 311).

   "The Prophet taught very clearly that man is in very deed the offspring of God, and that the spirits of men were born in the spirit world the children of God." (See *Teachings of the Prophet Joseph Smith*, p. 158, footnote 5, and pp. 352–53.)

4. T See 3, above. Apostle John A. Widsoe said, "The eternal ego of man was, in some past age of the other world, dim to us, clothed with a spiritual body. That was man's spiritual birth and his entrance into the spiritual world. Then later, on earth, . . . he will receive a material body. The term *an intelligence* is then applied to the eternal ego existing even before the spiritual creation. In reading Latter-day literature, the two-fold sense in which the terms *an intelligence* or *intelligences* are used—applied to spiritual personages or to pre-spiritual entities—must be carefully kept in mind" (*Evidences and Reconciliations*, 3:74–77, 1951).

5. T Heavenly Father has a body of flesh and bone (D&C 130:22). We understand from the following quote that both Heavenly Father and Heavenly Mother have glorified resurrected bodies of flesh and bone. "Only resurrected and glorified beings can become parents of spirit offspring. Only such exalted souls have reached maturity in the appointed course of eternal life; and the spirits born to them in the eternal worlds will pass in

due sequence through the several stages or estates by which the glorified parents have attained exaltation." (This is a quote from President Joseph F. Smith, *Gospel Doctrine,* p. 70.)

6. ? This could be either true or false, depending on how technical you get. It is true, in a general sense, that resurrected bodies produce spirit offspring (see 5, above); however, only those in the highest degree of the celestial kingdom will use the powers of procreation to bring forth spirit children. (See D&C 131:1–4.) Joseph Fielding Smith taught, "Some of the functions in the celestial body will not appear in the terrestrial body, neither in the telestial body, and the power of procreation will be removed" (*Doctrines of Salvation*, Vol. II, p. 288).

7. T Acts 17:28–29 says, "We are also his offspring . . . we are the offspring of God." President Joseph F. Smith, John R. Winder and Anthon H. Lund, as the First Presidency, said, "All men and women are in the similitude of the universal Father and Mother and are literally the sons and daughters of Deity" (James R. Clark, *Messages of the First Presidency*, 4:203).

8. F See number 3, above. If you want to be technical, it could be "true" in the sense that spirit is actual matter (D&C 131:7–8), and so the matter from which your spirit body was created has always existed. But your spirit body came into existence when you were born to Heavenly Parents.

9. T D&C 131:7–8

10. T See Ether 3:6, where the brother of Jared sees the "finger of the Lord," which "was as the finger of a man, like unto flesh and blood." See also Ether 3:16, where the premortal Christ told him that he was seeing "the body of my spirit."

"Our spirit bodies had their beginning in pre-existence when we were born as the spirit children of God our Father . . . The bodies so created have all the parts of mortal bodies" (*Mormon Doctrine*, p. 750). A quote from the *Doctrines of the Gospel Student Manual* is also helpful on this: "It [the spirit body] possesses, in fact, all the organs and parts exactly corresponding to the outward tabernacle [i.e., physical body]."

(*Doctrines of the Gospel Student Manual*, Institutes of Religion, Religion 431–432, 2004, p. 14).

11. F This rumor has been around for a long time. It is not documented by authoritative sources and therefore must be considered false. This rumor may come from peoples' interpretation of scriptures such as Isaiah 14:12, where Satan is referred to as "Lucifer, son of the morning." Doctrine and Covenants 76:26 refers to him as "a" son of the morning, not "the" son of the morning. Or, people might be reading Abraham 3:28, which says "the second [Satan] was angry," meaning the second one to volunteer to be our Redeemer, not the second one born. So, we don't know when Satan was born into the premortal spirit world.

12. F We know that we developed at different rates. The Savior is our Elder Brother and is far ahead of us. Also, obvious differences show up in us as we come through the veil into mortality. (See Abraham 3:19 and 22 and Alma 13.)

13. F "There were no neutrals in the war in heaven. All took sides, either with Christ or with Satan" (*Doctrines of Salvation*, Joseph Fielding Smith, Vol. I, p. 66). Obviously, some may have taken longer to make up their minds as to which one to follow, but ultimately, all had to choose.

14. F Spirits cannot be killed. It was a war of words, philosophies, true and false doctrines, etc., and is still going on here on earth. Of course, you could have answered "true" if you were thinking "spiritual death," i.e., being cast out with Satan and permanently cut off from the presence of God. (See D&C 29:41; Helaman 14:18; and Alma 12:16.)

15. T See Abraham 3:22–24. Joseph Fielding Smith said, "It is true that Adam helped to form this earth. He labored with our Savior Jesus Christ. I have a strong view or conviction that there were others also who assisted them. Perhaps Noah and Enoch; and why not Joseph Smith, and those who were appointed to be rulers before the earth was formed?" (*Doctrines of Salvation*, Vol. I, pp. 74–75).

16. T Revelation 12:4, 7–9; 2 Nephi 9:9; D&C 29:36–39.

17. ? You could answer either way, depending on what you are thinking. It is true that Satan and his evil spirits can tempt people in the spirit world, but only in the prison portion. "When the righteous saints go to paradise, they will no longer be tempted, but the wicked in hell are subject to the control and torments of Lucifer" (*Mormon Doctrine*, p. 782). (See also priesthood and Relief Society lesson manual, *Teachings of the Presidents of the Church, Brigham Young*, p. 282.)

18. F "That world [the spirit world] is upon this earth" (*Mormon Doctrine*, p. 762, quoting from *Teachings of the Prophet Joseph Smith*, p. 326, and *Discourses of Brigham Young*, p. 376).

19. T Alma 40:11–14; 1 Peter 3:18–19.

20. ? It depends on how technical you want to be in answering this question. In the general sense, it is true. However, all children who die before the years of accountability go to paradise. Therefore, you could say the answer is false.

As far as all others are concerned, Joseph Fielding Smith said (speaking of the spirit world), "There, as I understand it, the righteous—meaning those who have been baptized and who have been faithful—are gathered in one part and all the others in another part of the spirit world." Elder Smith also said that the unrighteous "included all the spirits not baptized" (*Doctrines of Salvation*, Vol. II, p. 230; see also priesthood and Relief Society lesson manual, *Teachings of the Presidents of the Church, Brigham Young*, 1997, p. 282).

21. F Alma 34:34 tells us that people will still be basically the same when they enter the spirit world, so "instant conversions" probably won't happen very often.

22. T See *Doctrines of Salvation*, Joseph Fielding Smith, Vol. I, p. 60, for a discussion of why we are not able to remember our former life.

23. T In "The Family: A Proclamation to the World" (*Ensign*, November 2010, p. 129), The First Presidency and Quorum of the Twelve said, "All human beings—male and female—are created in the image of God. Each is a beloved spirit son or daughter of Heavenly Parents."

24. T In 1918, President Joseph F. Smith said, "The Spirit of Jesus Christ was full grown before he was born into the world; and so our children were full grown and possessed their full stature in the spirit, before they entered mortality, the same stature they will possess after they have passed away from mortality, and as they will also appear after the resurrection, when they shall have completed their mission" (*Gospel Doctrine*, Deseret Book, 1997, p. 455).

25. T "If you see one of your children that has passed away it may appear to you in the form in which you would recognize it, the form of childhood; but if it came to you as a messenger bearing some important truth, it would perhaps come as the spirit of Bishop Edward Hunter's son (who died when a little child) came to him, in the stature of full-grown manhood, and revealed himself to his father, and said: 'I am your son' " (ibid.).

26. T "The mortal estate in which we find ourselves is absolutely necessary to our exaltation" (Joseph Fielding Smith, *Doctrines of Salvation*, Vol. I, p. 91).

27. T See Doctrine and Covenants 131:1–4 and 132:16–17. Joseph Fielding Smith said, referring to those who go to the terrestrial and telestial kingdoms, "In both of these kingdoms there will be changes in the bodies and limitations. They will not have the power of increase, neither the power or nature to live as husbands and wives, for this will be denied them and they cannot increase. Those who receive the exaltation in the celestial kingdom will have the 'continuation of the seeds forever' (D&C 132:19). They will live in the family relationship. In the terrestrial and in the telestial kingdoms there will be no marriage. Those who enter there will remain 'separately and singly' forever" (*Doctrines of Salvation*, Vol. II, p. 287).

28. T See answer #27, above.

29. T Doctrine and Covenants 132:20 and 22. See also Brigham Young as follows: "After men have got their exaltations and their crowns and have become Gods . . . they have the power

then of propagating their species in spirit; and that is the first of their operations with regard to organizing a world" (*Journal of Discourses*, 6:275).

30. F Innumerable people will make it. (See D&C 76:67 and Revelation 7:9.) This is encouraging.

31. F He will wear red (Isaiah 63:2; D&C 133:48), but it will represent the blood of the wicked who will be destroyed at His coming (D&C 133:51).

32. F "In the resurrection, there will be different kinds of bodies; they will not all be alike. The body a man receives will determine his place hereafter. There will be celestial bodies, terrestrial bodies, and telestial bodies, and these bodies will differ" (*Doctrines of Salvation*, Joseph Fielding Smith, Vol. II, p. 286; see also 1 Corinthians 15:39–42; D&C 88:28–32; and answer #27, above).

33. T Telestial people will not be resurrected until the end of the Millennium (D&C 88:100–101).

34. F Isaiah 65:20 says people will live to be one hundred years old. Joseph Fielding Smith, speaking of life during the Millennium, said, "A change, nevertheless, will come over all who remain on the earth; they will be quickened so that they will not be subject unto death until they are old. Men shall die when they are one hundred years of age" (*The Way to Perfection*, pp. 298–99; see also *Doctrines of the Gospel Student Manual*, p. 104).

35. ? Depends on how specific you are thinking. Obviously, at the beginning of the Millennium, there will be no wicked, because they all will have been destroyed. The Millennium will be a time of peace; however, people will still have agency. Thus, Isaiah 65:20 indicates that there will be an occasional sinner during the Millennium who will be accursed at the end of his or her one hundred years.

36. F President Joseph Fielding Smith taught concerning the binding of Satan: "There are many among us who teach that the binding of Satan will be merely the binding which those dwelling on the earth will place upon him by their refusal to hear his enticings. This is not so. He will not have the privilege during that period

of time to tempt any man (D&C 101:28)" (*Church History and Modern Revelation*, 1:192; see also *Doctrine and Covenants Student Manual*, Religion 324–325, p. 89).

37. T "Physical bodies of those living on earth during the Millennium will not be subject to the same ills that attend us in our present sphere of existence. Men in that day will still be mortal . . . But their bodies will be changed from conditions as they now exist so that disease cannot attack them, and death as we know it cannot intervene to cause a separation of body and spirit" (*Mormon Doctrine*, pp. 497–98).

38. F This is false doctrine. Doctrine and Covenants 137:10 tells us that children who die before the age of accountability "are saved in the celestial kingdom of heaven." People who live during the Millennium will live to one hundred years old (Isaiah 65:20) and then be "twinkled," i.e., resurrected into a body that represents the kingdom they will receive (see also D&C 88:28–32).

39. T The First Presidency of the Church said, "Only resurrected and glorified [exalted] beings can become parents of spirit offspring. Only such exalted souls have reached maturity in the appointed course of eternal life; and the spirits born to them in the eternal worlds will pass in due sequence through the several stages or estates by which the glorified parents have attained exaltation" (First Presidency Statement, *Improvement Era*, August 1916, p. 942).

If you took the True-False Quiz, checked your answers using the answer key, and learned as needed from the answers given, you already have a pretty good knowledge of the plan of salvation. We will now look at a brief overview of the plan.

THUMBNAIL SKETCH OF THE PLAN OF SALVATION (ALMA 42:5)

- Premortality
  - Intelligence
  - Spirit Birth
  - War in Heaven

- Creation
- Fall
- Atonement
- Mortality
- Postmortal Spirit World
  - Paradise
  - Prison
- Second Coming
- Millennium
- Little Season—Battle of Gog and Magog
- Final Judgment
  - Three Degrees of Glory
    - Celestial
    - Terrestrial
    - Telestial
  - Perdition (Outer Darkness)
- Then What?

Here is a simple chart representing the plan of salvation.

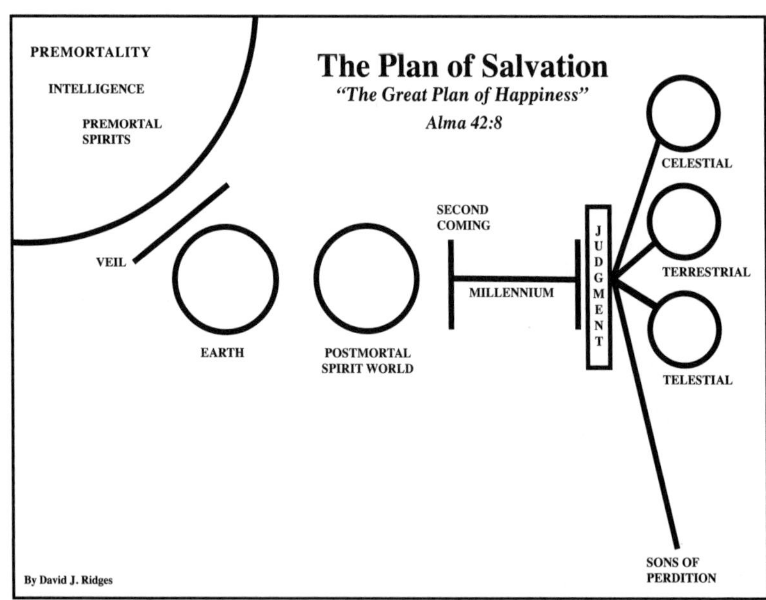

We will now briefly discuss the various stages of the plan of salvation and include many of the questions asked by my students through the years in my classes.

PREMORTALITY

The first stage is what we call "premortality," meaning our existence before we became mortal through physical birth on this earth. There were two major stages in premortality—intelligence and spirit birth.

INTELLIGENCE

The first thing we know about ourselves is that we existed as intelligence before we were born as spirits to Heavenly Parents.

Q: How long did we exist as intelligence?
A: Forever.

> D&C 93:29
>
> Intelligence, or the light of truth, was not created or made, neither indeed can be.

So, we know that we have existed forever. While that fact may boggle our minds a bit, it is important that we be aware of it.

Q: What is intelligence?
A: We don't know.

In fact, we don't even know whether to refer to this stage of our eternal journey as "intelligence" or "intelligences." Sometimes it is as important to know that we don't have an answer as it is to understand what has been revealed. If we stick with what we know and don't spend much time speculating about what has not been revealed, it can keep us from going off the deep end, sometimes losing our testimonies in the process. Some people lose their way by engaging in too much study of so-called "mysteries." Joseph Fielding Smith, who became the tenth

President of the Church, gave us good counsel regarding our premortal existence as intelligence.

> The intelligent part of man was not created, but always existed. There has been some speculation and articles have been written attempting to explain just what these "**intelligences**" are, or this "**intelligence**" is, but it is futile for us to speculate upon it. We do know that intelligence was not created or made and cannot be because the Lord has said it. There are some truths it is well to leave until the Lord sees fit to reveal the fulness. (Joseph Fielding Smith, *Church History and Modern Revelation,* 1:401; see also *Doctrines of the Gospel Student Manual,* Religion 430 and 431, 2004, p. 13)

Q: How long will we continue to exist after we leave this life?
A: Forever.

The scriptures are clear on this. Jacob, Nephi's brother, taught us that we will live forever.

> 2 Nephi 9:13
>
> 13 O how great the plan of our God! . . . **the spirit and the body is restored to itself again, and all men become incorruptible, and immortal.**

Did you know that one of Satan's prime goals is to destroy the idea in our minds that we are eternal beings? Why would he want people to believe that they are not eternal beings? Answer: for many reasons, such as

- If there is no life after death, it really doesn't matter what you do in this life.
- If no life after death, there is no accountability.
- If no life after this one, we have no value or real worth, and neither does anyone else.

Q: Is it possible to cease to exist completely?
A: No.

Even sons of perdition will continue to exist forever according to Doctrine and Covenants 88:32.

I had a student come into my office once and ask if I knew of a sin that she could commit that would cause her to completely cease to exist. She said she knew that we have three basic components of our beings; namely, intelligence, spirit body, and physical body. She continued that she knew that if she took her own life it wouldn't do her any good, because she'd still continue to exist as a spirit in the postmortal spirit world. (She had a pretty good knowledge of things!) What she wanted was something she could do or a sin she could commit that would cause her intelligence, spirit, and physical body to be completely exterminated so she would truly cease to exist. There is no such thing. That answer, which is absolute fact, left her frustrated. What she really wanted was to completely avoid accountability for some sins she was currently involved in. As we continued to chat, I recommended that she talk to her bishop. She finally agreed to do so. She worked things out, repented successfully, and went on to appreciate life, including a temple marriage and family. The Atonement of Christ was her answer, as it is ours.

SPIRIT BIRTH

Q: When did we become spirit beings?

A: In premortality when we were born as spirit children to our Heavenly Parents.

So, at the time of our birth as spirits, our intelligence was clothed with a spirit body. President Spencer W. Kimball taught this simple truth as follows:

> God is your father. He loves you. **He and your mother in heaven** value you beyond any measure. They **gave your eternal intelligence spirit form, just as your earthly mother and father have given you a mortal body**. You are unique. One of a kind, made of the eternal intelligence which gives you claim upon eternal life. (President Spencer W. Kimball, *Ensign*, November 1978, p. 105)

The Apostle Paul explains clearly in the Bible that we are the **offspring** of God, His spirit children.

Acts 17:29

29 Forasmuch then as **we are the offspring of God**, we ought not to think that the Godhead is like unto gold, or silver, or stone, graven by art and man's device [*in other words, since we are offspring of God, we shouldn't think He is some kind of graven image or idol*].

A statement by the First Presidency of the Church in 1925 clearly taught this beautiful doctrine:

> **Man, as a spirit**, was **begotten** [conceived] and **born** of **Heavenly Parents**, and **reared to maturity** in the eternal mansions of the Father, **prior to coming upon the earth.** (The First Presidency, Heber J. Grant and counselors, "The Mormon View of Evolution," *Improvement Era,* September, 1925)

Q: Is spirit a form of actual matter?
A: Yes.

D&C 131:7

7 There is no such thing as immaterial matter. **All spirit is matter**, but it is more fine or pure, and can only be discerned by purer eyes.

Q: Do our spirit bodies have the same parts that our mortal bodies have? In other words, were we "real people" as spirits in premortality?
A: Yes.

> Our *spirit bodies* had their beginning in pre-existence when we were born as the spirit children of God our Father . . . **The bodies so created have all the parts of mortal bodies.** (Bruce R. McConkie, *Mormon Doctrine*, Bookcraft, 1966, p. 750)

THE WAR IN HEAVEN

The Bible teaches that there was a "war in heaven."

Revelation 12:7–9

7 And there was **war in heaven**: Michael [*the premortal Adam*] and his angels [*the righteous in premortality*] fought against the dragon [*Lucifer, the devil*]; and the dragon fought and his angels [*the spirits who followed Satan*],

8 And prevailed not [*didn't win*]; neither was their place found any more in heaven.

9 And **the great dragon was cast out**, that old serpent, called the Devil, and Satan, which deceiveth the whole world: **he was cast out into the earth, and his angels were cast out with him**.

Q: What kind of a war was it?
A: A battle for our souls and our loyalty.

Spirits cannot be killed or injured, so it wasn't the kind of war we are used to here on earth. Therefore, this would have been a war of words, ideas, truth versus falsehood, philosophies, etc. In other words, it was a battle for our loyalty, our minds, and our use of moral agency. President Gordon B. Hinckley spoke in reference to the War in Heaven. He taught,

> The book of Revelation speaks briefly of what must have been a terrible conflict for the **minds and loyalties** of God's children. (President Gordon B. Hinckley, General Conference, April 6, 2003)

Q: Was the War in Heaven concluded at that time?
A: No. It is still continuing here on earth now.

Q: When will it be finished?
A: At the end of the "little season" after the end of the Millennium.

Thus, this battle for our souls and loyalty, which started with the war in heaven, will continue until it is concluded after the Millennium at the end of the Battle of Gog and Magog. This final battle, during which the war in heaven is finally concluded, is described briefly in the Doctrine and Covenants as follows, starting with when the devil is let loose at the end of the Millennium after having been bound and unable to tempt the children of God on earth for a thousand years.

D&C 88:111–15

111 And then he shall be loosed for a little season, that he may gather together his armies.

112 And Michael [*Adam*], the seventh angel, even the archangel, shall gather together his armies, even the hosts of heaven.

113 And the devil shall gather together his armies; even the hosts of hell, and shall come up to battle against Michael and his armies.

114 And then cometh the battle of the great God [*the battle of Gog and Magog; see Bible Dictionary, under "Gog"*]; and **the devil and his armies shall be cast away into their own place, that they shall not have power over the saints any more at all**.

115 For Michael shall fight their battles, and shall overcome him [*the devil, Lucifer*] who seeketh the throne of him who sitteth upon the throne, even the Lamb [*Christ*].

CREATION

Q: Who Created the earth?
A: The premortal Jesus Christ under the direction of the Father.

Moses 1:32–33

32 And **by the word of my power** [*in other words, through Christ*], **have I** [*the Father*] **created them** [*this world, as well as countless others*], **which is mine Only Begotten Son**, who is full of grace and truth.

33 And **worlds without number have I created**; and I also created them for mine own purpose; and **by the Son I created them**, which is mine Only Begotten.

Q: How long did it take to create the earth?
A: We don't know.

A common answer is six thousand years. Another often-heard answer is millions of years. The fact is, we don't know. It hasn't been revealed yet. Apostle Bruce R. McConkie reminded us that we don't know.

> But first, what is a day? It is a specified time period; it is an age, an eon, a division of eternity; it is the time between two identifiable events. And each day, of whatever length, has the duration needed for its purposes. . . . **There is no revealed recitation specifying that each of the "six days" involved in the creation was of the same duration.** (*Doctrines of the Gospel Student Manual,* 2000 edition, p. 17)

Q: Where was it created?
A: Near the planet where Heavenly Father lives.

Brigham Young taught,

> **When the earth was framed and brought into existence and man was placed upon it, it was near the throne of our Father in heaven.** And when man fell . . . **the earth fell into space, and took up its abode in this planetary system**, and the sun became our light . . . This is the glory the earth came from, and when it is glorified **it will return again unto the presence of the Father**, and it will dwell there. (*Journal of Discourses,* 26 vols. [London: Latter-day Saints' Book Depot, 1854–1886], Vol. 17, p. 143)

Q: When will we get more information about the creation?
A: When the Savior comes.

It is important that we do not get caught up in arguments or speculation as to how long it actually took to create the earth. We do know for sure that the Lord created it. Jesus will give us more details about the creation of the earth when He comes again, as stated in the Doctrine and Covenants as follows:

D&C 101:32–33

32 Yea, verily I say unto you, in that day **when the Lord shall come, he shall reveal all things**—

33 Things which have passed, and hidden things which no man knew, **things of the earth, by which it was made**, and the purpose and the end thereof—

Q: Did we evolve from lower forms of life?
A: No, according to the First Presidency.

It is held by some that Adam was not the first man upon this earth, and that the original human being was a development from lower orders of the animal creation. These, however, are the theories of men. The word of the Lord declares that Adam was "the first man of all men" (Moses 1:34), and we are therefore in duty bound to regard him as the primal parent of our race . . . **Man began life as a human being, in the likeness of our heavenly Father.** (The First Presidency, Joseph F. Smith, John R. Winder, and Anthon H. Lund, *Improvement Era*, November 1909, 13:75–61)

THE FALL OF ADAM AND EVE

Q: What was the Fall?
A: When Adam and Eve partook of the forbidden fruit and were cast out of the Garden of Eden.

Q: Was the Fall good or bad?
A: Good.

It is sometimes said that Adam and Eve "fell forward." In other words, it was a vital part of the Father's plan for us. We owe them a great debt of gratitude for doing it. Without the Fall, we wouldn't be here to ask questions about it. This fact is included in the following scriptural summary of the Fall:

2 Nephi 2:22–25

22 And now, behold, **if Adam had not transgressed he would not have fallen**, but he would have remained in the garden of Eden. **And all things** which were created **must have** [*would have*] **remained in the same state** in which they were after they were created; and they must have remained **forever**, and had no end.

23 And they would have had **no children**; wherefore they would have remained in a state of innocence, having **no joy**, for they knew **no misery**; doing **no good**, for they knew no sin.

24 But behold**, all things have been done in the wisdom of him who knoweth all things** [*in other words, this was part of God's plan for us*].

25 **Adam fell that men might be; and men are, that they might have joy**.

Q: What were the two main commandments given to Adam and Eve in the Garden of Eden?
A: To have children and not eat the forbidden fruit.

Genesis 1:28

28 And God blessed them, and God said unto them, **Be fruitful, and multiply, and replenish the earth** [*in other words, have children*], and subdue it: and have dominion over the fish of the sea, and over the fowl of the air, and over every living thing that moveth upon the earth.

Genesis 2:17

17 **But of the tree of the knowledge of good and evil** [*in other words, the forbidden fruit*], **thou shalt not eat** of it: for in the day that thou eatest thereof thou shalt surely die.

These two commandments are often referred to as the "two conflicting commandments." You know, "Have children but don't eat the forbidden fruit so you can become mortal and have children." To many

Christians, it appears that God was a bit unfair, giving commandments where Adam and Eve couldn't keep the one without breaking the other. So . . .

Q: What about the two "conflicting commandments?"
A: They are not "conflicting" if you know the rest of the story.

In the following two quotes, Joseph Fielding Smith gives "the rest of the story" regarding the seemingly conflicting commandments:

> Now this is the way I interpret that: The Lord said to Adam, here is the Tree of the Knowledge of Good and Evil. **If you want to stay here, then you cannot eat of that fruit. If you want to stay here, then I forbid you to eat it. But you may act for yourself, and you may eat of it if you want to. And if you eat it, you will die**. (Joseph Fielding Smith, "Charge to Religious Educators," p. 124, quoted in *Doctrines of the Gospel Student Manual*, 2000 Edition, p. 20)

Just why the Lord would say to Adam that he forbade him to partake of the fruit of that tree is not made clear in the Bible account, **but in the original, as it comes to us in the Book of Moses, it is made definitely clear. It is that the Lord said to Adam that if he wished to remain as he was in the garden, then he was not to eat the fruit, but if he desired to eat it and partake of death, he was at liberty to do so**. So really, it was not in the true sense a transgression of a divine commandment. Adam made the wise decision. In fact, he made the only decision that he could make.

It was the divine plan from the very beginning that man should be placed on the earth and be subject to mortal conditions and pass through a probationary state (see Joseph Fielding Smith, *Answers to Gospel Questions*, vol. 4, p. 81).

Q: What are the main benefits of the Fall for us?
A: There are many.

<u>Briefly</u>

- We get to come to earth.
- We get a physical body, which is far better than just being a spirit.

- We get to personally experience joy, misery, good, evil, comfort, pain, etc.
- We get to experience opposition and temptation in a mortal environment.
- We get to exercise moral agency in a mortal "classroom."

Q: Was it fair to Adam and Eve to have to make such a choice without all the facts?

A: Of course! It has to be, because God is completely fair. If He were not, He couldn't be God.

The above answer is one of the most important facts you will ever learn. God is indeed completely fair. Otherwise, He would cease to be God, as stated in Alma 42:13, 22, and 25. So, it is clear that He is completely fair with everyone and that He was completely fair with Adam and Eve. It helps to know that even though they were "innocent" in the Garden, that does not mean that they had no knowledge. Babies and young children are innocent until the age of accountability (eight years of age—see D&C 68:25, 27), but, as you well know, they have a lot of knowledge with which they make many choices.

So, knowing full well that God is completely fair, it is obvious that the complete account of the temptation of Adam and Eve in the Garden of Eden is not contained in the Bible. Apostle John A. Widtsoe fills in some important details as follows:

> Such was the problem before our first parents: to remain forever at selfish ease in the Garden of Eden, or to face unselfishly tribulation and death, in bringing to pass the purposes of the Lord for a host of waiting spirit children. They chose the latter . . . **This they did with open eyes and minds as to consequences**. The memory of their former estates [*including their premortal spirit existence*] may have been dimmed, **but the gospel had been taught them during their sojourn in the Garden of Eden** . . . the choice that they made raises Adam and Eve to preeminence among all who have come on earth. (John A. Widtsoe, *Evidences and Reconciliations*, pp. 193–94)

THE ATONEMENT OF CHRIST

The Creation, Fall, and Atonement go together. They are inseparable if one desires to understand the Father's plan of salvation for us. We have discussed the Creation and the Fall. Now we will complete the package by discussing the Atonement of Jesus Christ.

The Atonement is the central focus of the plan of salvation. It has been active in our lives all the way from premortality to the present and will continue to bless and assist us through our final judgment and on into eternity as we continue progressing toward exaltation. Exaltation means literally becoming like our Father in Heaven; or, in other words, becoming gods. The Savior's Atonement gives us a "perfect brightness of hope" (2 Nephi 31:20) that we can make it, as long as we sincerely strive to live in harmony with the gospel.

Q: What is the Atonement?
A: The Savior's suffering for our sins in the Garden of Gethsemane and on the cross, His crucifixion, death, and resurrection.

In *True to the Faith*, published by the Church in 2004, page 17, we read,

> Jesus's atoning sacrifice took place in the Garden of Gethsemane and on the cross at Calvary. In Gethsemane He submitted to the will of the Father and began to take upon Himself the sins of all people . . . The Savior continued to suffer for our sins when He allowed Himself to be crucified . . . Through His death and Resurrection, He overcame physical death for us all.

Q: What are the most basic results of the Atonement?
A: Part 1. Resurrection for everyone, regardless of lifestyle.

<u>1 Corinthians 15:22</u>

22 For as in Adam all die, even so in Christ shall **all be made alive**.

2 Nephi 9:22

22 And he suffereth this **that the resurrection might pass upon all men**, that all might stand before him at the great and judgment day.

Thus, the Savior's Atonement, which includes His resurrection, overcomes physical death for everyone who has ever been born or will be born on earth. This includes everyone, even those who become sons of perdition (D&C 88:32).

A: Part 2. The opportunity, through living the gospel, to be forgiven of sins and, ultimately, gain exaltation.

The second major part of the Atonement, being saved from our sins, requires that we exercise our agency and repent of our sins. It is important to understand that true repentance enables the Savior's Atonement to free us completely from the effects of sin.

Isaiah 1:18

18 Come now, and let us reason together, saith the Lord: **though your sins be as scarlet, they shall be as white as snow**; though they be red like crimson, they shall be as wool.

D&C 58:42–43

42 Behold, **he who has repented of his sins, the same is forgiven, and I, the Lord, remember them no more**.

43 By this ye may know if a man repenteth of his sins—behold, he will confess them and forsake them.

Recently, I heard a false doctrine to the effect that all our sins will be brought up on Judgment Day, even the ones we have repented of, so that everyone will see evidence that the Atonement works and that God is merciful. Ouch! That's terrible! Verse 42, above, clearly tells us that our sins that we have properly repented of will not even be brought up on Judgment Day.

Q: What are some other benefits of the Atonement?

A: The Savior took upon Himself our infirmities, inadequacies, pains, sicknesses, and so forth, including stupid things we do, so that we can have His help in overcoming all things that stand in our way to attaining exaltation. It thus also helps us live much more satisfying and happy lives here in mortality.

Alma 7:11–12

11 And he shall go forth, suffering pains and afflictions and temptations of every kind; and this that the word might be fulfilled which saith **he will take upon him the pains and the sicknesses of his people**.

12 And **he will take upon him death, that he may loose the bands of death** which bind his people; and **he will take upon him their infirmities**, that his bowels may be filled with mercy, according to the flesh, that he may know according to the flesh how to succor his people according to their infirmities.

Elder Neal A. Maxwell taught this as follows:

In Alma 7:12, the only place in scriptures, to my knowledge, that it appears, there seems to have been yet another purpose of the Atonement, speaking again of the Savior and his suffering, "And he will take upon him death, that he may loose the bands of death which bind his people; and he will take upon him their infirmities, that his bowels may be filled with mercy, according to his flesh, that he may know according to the flesh, how to succor his people according to their infirmities." Have you ever thought that there was no way that Jesus could know the suffering which we undergo as a result of our stupidity and sin (because he was sinless) except he bear those sins of ours in what I call the awful arithmetic of the Atonement? And according to this prophet, Jesus now knows, according to the flesh, how to succor us and how to help us as a result of that suffering, which knowledge could have come in no other way. (Neal A. Maxwell, "The Old Testament: Relevancy within Antiquity," *A Symposium on the Old Testament*, p. 17; see also *Doctrines of the Gospel Student Manual*, 1986, pp. 24–25)

Q: What are some important vocabulary terms for understanding the Atonement?

A: Here is a basic list:

Physical Death

The temporary separation of the body and spirit at the time of mortal death.

Resurrection

The permanent reuniting of the spirit and body.

Spiritual death

Being cast out of the direct presence of God, as was the case with Adam and Eve after the Fall. It also refers to anyone who ultimately loses the privilege of returning to the presence of God to live eternally.

Justice

The law of justice requires that all sins be paid for, whether by Christ's Atonement or by individuals themselves.

Mercy

The law of mercy allows Christ's Atonement to pay for our sins and thus satisfy the requirements of the Law of Justice, if we repent. Thus, we can be made clean and free from sin, worthy to enter the presence of God and enabled to continue progressing until we become gods.

Q: How many times can we repent?

A: The answer is found in the Book of Mormon.

Mosiah 26:30

30 Yea, and **as often as my people repent will I forgive them** their trespasses against me.

Q: Does the Atonement of Jesus Christ apply to our world alone, or to other worlds also?

A: Other worlds also.

D&C 76:24

24 That **by him** [*Christ*], and through him, and of him, the **worlds** [*note that this is plural*] are and were created, and **the inhabitants thereof** [*of all the Father's worlds*] **are begotten sons and daughters unto God** [*are given the opportunity to gain exaltation*].

MORTALITY

We are here. We are experiencing mortality. Our intelligence was clothed with a body of spirit in premortality, and now our spirit has been clothed with a physical, mortal body. It is all part of the plan.

Q: Why is a physical body so important?
A: Without one we cannot become like our Heavenly Father.

As spirit children of God in our premortal life, one of the things we most admired and strongly desired was a glorified, resurrected physical body of flesh and bones, like the one Heavenly Father has. Obtaining a physical body here on earth by means of mortal birth is a required step in the Father's plan for us to become like Him.

Q: What are some other purposes of mortal life?
A: There are many, including

- Learn to have joy (2 Nephi 2:25)
- Be tested (Abraham 3:25)
- Experience opposition (2 Nephi 2:11–14)
- Learn to appreciate the good by tasting the bitter (2 Nephi 2:15, 23)
- Learn to walk by faith (Galatians 2:20; Romans 1:17; D&C 88:118)
- Use the Atonement in our daily lives to continue growing and progressing (2 Nephi 31:20)

POSTMORTAL SPIRIT WORLD

The postmortal spirit world is where everyone goes when they die. It has two divisions spoken of in the scriptures:

Paradise (Alma 40:12) (a place to continue preparing for celestial glory and exaltation)

Prison (1 Peter 3:19) (the spirit world mission field)

Q: Where is the postmortal spirit world?
A: On this earth.

Brigham Young taught,

> When you lay down this tabernacle, where are you going? Into the spiritual world . . . **Where is the spirit world? It is right here.** (*Discourses of Brigham Young*, Deseret Book, 1954, p. 376)

Joseph Smith mentioned those who have died. He said,

> Enveloped in flaming fire, **they are not far from us**, and know and understand our thoughts, feelings, and motions, and are often pained therewith." (*Teachings of the Prophet Joseph Smith*, 1977, p. 326)

Q: Who goes to paradise?
A: Faithful, baptized members of the Church, plus babies and children who die before the age of accountability (8 years old—see D&C 68:27).

> **Paradise** . . . designates **a place of peace and happiness in the postmortal spirit world**, reserved for those who have been baptized and who have remained faithful (see Alma 40:12 and Moroni 10:34). (*True to the Faith*, The Church of Jesus Christ of Latter-day Saints, 2004, p. 111)

D&C 137:10

10 And I also beheld that **all children who die before they arrive at the years of accountability are saved in the celestial kingdom of heaven.**

Q: Who goes to prison (the spirit world mission field)?

A: Everyone else, including those who are wicked when they die and also good people who have not yet had a fair chance to hear and accept or reject the gospel at the time of their death.

You can see from the following quote about spirit prison that the environment there is quite similar to the world in which we live. I prefer to call it "the spirit world mission field."

> Spirit Prison: The Apostle Peter referred to the postmortal spirit world as a prison, which it is for some (see 1 Peter 3:18–20). In the spirit prison are the spirits of those who have not yet received the gospel of Jesus Christ. These spirits have agency and may be enticed by both good and evil. If they accept the gospel and the ordinances performed for them in the temples, they may leave the spirit prison and dwell in paradise. (*Gospel Principles,* The Church of Jesus Christ of Latter-day Saints, 2009, p. 244)

Q: Why is it called "prison"?

A: Because people there are limited since they don't have the gospel in their lives.

Q: Why is spirit prison sometimes referred to as "Hell"?

A: Because it is, for some of the people who go there.

> Also in the spirit prison are those who rejected the gospel after it was preached to them either on earth or in the spirit prison. These spirits suffer in a condition known as hell. They have removed themselves from the mercy of Jesus Christ. . . . After suffering for their sins, they will be allowed, through the Atonement of Jesus Christ, to inherit the lowest degree of glory, which is the telestial kingdom. (*Gospel Principles,* The Church of Jesus Christ of Latter-day Saints, 2009, p. 244)

Q: Can Satan and his evil spirits tempt in the postmortal spirit world?
A: Yes and no.

They can tempt in the spirit prison (spirit world mission field) just as they tempt people here on earth, but they cannot tempt the righteous spirits who have gone to paradise. President Brigham Young said,

> If we are faithful to our religion, when we go into the spirit world, the fallen spirits—Lucifer and the third part of the heavenly hosts that came with him, and the spirits of wicked men who have dwelt upon this earth . . . will have no influence over our spirits . . . All the rest of the children of men are more or less subject to them, and they are subject to them as they were while here in the flesh. (Brigham Young, *Teachings of the Presidents of the Church, Brigham Young*, p. 282, Church study course for 2000)

Q: Who teaches the gospel in the spirit prison?
A: Faithful elders.

> D&C 138:57
>
> I beheld that the **faithful elders** of this dispensation, when they depart from mortal life, continue their labors in the preaching of the gospel of repentance and redemption, through the sacrifice of the Only Begotten Son of God, among those who are in darkness and under the bondage of sin in the great world of the spirits of the dead.

Q: Are there any sister missionaries teaching in spirit prison?
A: Absolutely!

> Now among all these millions of spirits that have lived on the earth and have passed away, . . . without the knowledge of the gospel—among them you may count that at least one-half are women. Who is going to preach the gospel to the women? . . . **these good sisters . . . will be fully authorized and empowered to preach the gospel and minister to the women while the elders and prophets are preaching it to the men.** (Joseph F. Smith, *Gospel Doctrine*, Deseret Book, 1977, p. 461)

THE SECOND COMING

The Savior's first coming was when He was born to Mary in Bethlehem. He came in humble circumstances and concluded His mortal mission and Atonement by suffering for our sins in the Garden of Gethsemane and on the cross; by giving His life through submitting to crucifixion; and through His resurrection, which completed His Atonement.

His Second Coming will be much different than the first. Everyone in the world and even those in the spirit world (Revelation 1:7) will see this coming. It is mentioned over fifteen hundred times in the Old Testament and some three hundred times in the New Testament. Members of the Church who understand the gospel are looking forward to the Second Coming, whether it takes place in their lifetime or later. When He comes, it will be with great power and glory. The righteous will be preserved, and the wicked will be burned as the earth is cleansed from wickedness and sin in preparation for the thousand-year Millennium.

Q: How do we know He is coming relatively soon?

A: The scriptures and modern prophets tell us, along with many "signs of the times" that are being fulfilled all around us.

Numerous scriptures inform us that the time of His coming is getting close, including many verses telling us what to look for as the time for His coming approaches. These prophecies are known as "signs of the times." Also, have you noticed that more and more general conference speakers lately are mentioning our role in preparing the earth for the Second Coming?

D&C 106:4

And again, verily I say unto you, **the coming of the Lord draweth nigh**, and it overtaketh the world as a thief in the night—

President Russell M. Nelson said the following:

My dear brethren, we have been given a sacred trust—the authority of God to bless others. May each one of us rise up as the man God foreordained us to be—ready to bear the priesthood of God bravely, eager to pay whatever price is required to increase his power in the priesthood. With *that* power, **we can help prepare the world for the Second Coming of our Savior, Jesus Christ**. This is His Church, led today by His prophet, President Thomas S. Monson, whom I dearly love and sustain. I so testify in the name of Jesus Christ, amen. (April General Conference, 2016, priesthood session)

Q: What are some of the "signs of the times"?

A: We will mention forty-four of them in a brief list here. There are more.

These are not necessarily listed in chronological order. The fulfillments of these prophecies mostly take place in the last days before the Second Coming; or, in other words, relatively late in the earth's six thousand years of mortal existence so far. By the way, our earth has a total of seven thousand years of temporal existence, according to Doctrine and Covenants 77:6, which would include the Millennium. So, it's clear that we live in the last days before the Second Coming of Christ.

1. There will be much despair, depression, emotional instability, and gloom and doom (Luke 21:25–27)
2. Jerusalem will be under siege (JS—Mathew 1:32; Bible Dictionary, p. 601)
3. A prophet named "Joseph" to be raised up (2 Nephi 3:11–15)
4. Coming forth of the Book of Mormon (Ezekiel 37:16–19)
5. Additional scriptures will come forth (Isaiah 29:11–12; 2 Nephi 27:6–20; Ezekiel 37:15–20; D&C 104:58–59)
6. Restoration of the priesthood (D&C 2:1; Malachi 4:5–6)
7. Restoration of the true Church (Acts 3:19–21)
8. The Church will grow to fill the whole earth (Daniel 2:35, 44–45)
9. Once restored in the last days, the true Church will never be lost again through apostasy (Daniel 2:44)
10. All will hear the gospel in their own language (D&C 90:10–11)
11. The name of Joseph Smith will be spoken of for good and evil in all nations (JS—History 1:33)

12. Scattered Israel will be gathered (1 Nephi 10:14; 1 Nephi 19:16; Isaiah 2:2–3; 6:13; Isaiah 5:26–30; D&C 39:11)
13. Lost ten tribes return (D&C 110:11; 133:26–34)
14. Times of the gentiles fulfilled (Luke 21:24; 1 Nephi 13:42; D&C 45:24–30)
15. Jews return to Jerusalem (D&C 45:24–25; 133:13)
16. Jews accept the true gospel (Zechariah 12:8–14; 13:6; 2 Nephi 30:7; D&C 45:51–53)
17. Elijah will come (Malachi 4:5–6)
18. Christ will come to His temple (Malachi 3:1; D&C 110:1–10)
19. Genealogical interest and research increases dramatically (Malachi 4:5–6; D&C 2:1–3)
20. Many in Egypt will accept the gospel and a temple will be built there (Isaiah 19:18–19, 21)
21. Diseases, plagues, pestilences sweep the earth (D&C 45:31; Joseph Smith—Matthew 1:29)
22. Wars and rumors of wars (Matthew 24:6; D&C 45:26; Joseph Smith—Matthew 1:23)
23. Famines, tornadoes, earthquakes, natural disasters to abound (D&C 45:33; 88:90)
24. Dangers in and upon the waters (D&C 61:4; 13–19)
25. Sexual immorality, homosexuality, and pornography everywhere (2 Timothy 3:3, 6; Helaman 4:12)
26. It will be common for couples to avoid marriage and openly live together (1 Timothy 4:1–3)
27. Much ecological damage will occur in the last days (Revelation 8:7–12; 16:2–4, 8, 17)
28. Many will openly approve of and advocate gross sin (Isaiah 5:20; Mormon 8:31)
29. Jerusalem to be a "cup of trembling" (a terror) to its enemies (Zechariah 12:2–3)

30. False churches and false prophets abound (Revelation 13:13–14); people admire and "worship" the influential wicked (Revelation 13:3–4).
31. Some of the "very elect" will be deceived (Joseph—Smith Matthew 1:22)
32. Lamanites to "blossom as the rose" (D&C 49:24)
33. New Jerusalem to be built (D&C 57:1–3; D&C 45:66–69; Moses 7:62–64; Ether 13:5–6)
34. Many temples to be built (President Benson and Elder Bruce R. McConkie, April General Conference, 1980)
35. Temple to be built in Jerusalem (*Teachings of the Prophet Joseph Smith*, p. 286; Ezekiel 37:26; *Doctrines of Salvation*, Vol. 2, p. 244)
36. The Constitution will hang by a thread (*Journal of Discourses*, Vol. 2, p. 182; Vol. 7, p. 15; President Ezra Taft Benson, "Our Divine Constitution," *Ensign*, November 1987, p. 4)
37. The Lord will hasten His work (D&C 88:73)
38. Battle of Armageddon (Zechariah 12; Revelation 16:16)
39. Meeting at Adam-ondi-Ahman (Daniel 7:9–14; D&C 27:5–14)
40. Two prophets killed in Jerusalem (Revelation 11; D&C 77:15)
41. Mount of Olives divides in two (Zechariah 14:4; D&C 45:48)
42. Righteous are taken up (D&C 88:96)
43. Wicked are burned (Malachi 4:1; 2 Nephi 12:10, 19, 21; D&C 5:19)
44. Everyone sees Christ coming (Revelation 1:7)

Q: Do we know for sure when He is coming?
A: No.

<u>Matthew 24:36</u>

36 **But of that day and hour knoweth no *man*,** no, not the angels of heaven, but my Father only.

Q: What will happen to the righteous when He comes?
A: They will be lifted up to meet Him as He comes.

D&C 88:96

96 And **the saints** that are upon the earth, who are alive, shall be quickened and be **caught up to meet him**.

Q: What will happen to the wicked?
A: They will be burned by the brightness of His glory.

2 Nephi 12:10

10 O **ye wicked ones**, enter into the rock, and hide thee in the dust, for the fear of the Lord and **the glory of his majesty shall smite thee**.

Q: What is the general dividing line between who survives His coming and who is destroyed?
A: Those who are living the basic standards required for entrance into the terrestrial and celestial kingdom will be spared. Those who are living sinful, unrepentant lives that would qualify them for the telestial kingdom or perdition will be burned.

Those whose lifestyles will qualify them for celestial glory include faithful, baptized members of the Church (D&C 76:51–53) and children who die before the years of accountability (D&C 137:10). Those whose lifestyles reflect the requirements for terrestrial glory include good and honorable people (D&C 76:71–80) who don't commit sins that would take them to telestial glory if they don't repent.

Those unrepentant sinners whose lifestyles will qualify them for telestial glory are described in Doctrine and Covenants 76:103, Revelation 22:15, and Galatians 5:19–21. The lifestyles and thinking of those who will qualify to be sons of perdition are described in Doctrine and Covenants 76:30–35.

Q: What color will Christ be wearing when He comes?
A: Red.

Whether the Savior's clothing is red literally, or red symbolically, the imagery is the same. The color represents the blood of the wicked who are destroyed at His Coming.

D&C 133:48, 51

48 **And the Lord shall be red in his apparel** [*clothing*], and his garments like him that treadeth in the wine-vat [*like one who has been treading grapes in the wine tub*].

51 And I have trampled them [*the wicked*] in my fury, and I did tread upon them in mine anger, and **their blood have I sprinkled upon my garments** [*clothing*]**, and stained all my raiment** [*clothing*]; for this was the day of vengeance [*the law of justice is being satisfied*] which was in my heart [*which is part of the plan of salvation, which the Savior is carrying out for the Father, along with the law of mercy*].

Q: What will happen to the earth?

A: The continents will be moved back together and the earth will be restored to a Garden of Eden-like condition (see footnote f in the tenth article of faith). In other words, it will receive its "paradisiacal glory" in preparation for the Millennium.

D&C 133:23

23 He shall command the great deep, and it shall be driven back into the north countries, and **the islands shall become one land**. [*All the continents will come together. There will be one continent and one ocean.*]

Tenth Article of Faith

10 We believe in the literal gathering of Israel and in the restoration of the Ten Tribes; that Zion (the New Jerusalem) will be built upon the American continent; that Christ will reign personally upon the earth; and, that **the earth will be renewed and receive its paradisiacal glory**.

MILLENNIUM

The Millennium is what we call the thousand years of peace on earth that is ushered in by the Lord's Second Coming. It will be a time of great accomplishment in the work of saving souls. Untold billions will be born and raised in righteousness, living as mortals on the "paradisiacal" earth (tenth article of faith) with Christ as the head of the worldwide government, ruling and reigning as "King of kings" (Revelation 17:14, 20:4). They will grow up, marry, raise families, and live until they are one hundred years old (Isaiah 65:20). Then they will die and be resurrected in "the twinkling of an eye" (D&C 101:31). Righteous, resurrected beings will be coming and going during the Millennium, helping with the work of saving souls, but the actual ordinance work for the dead will be done by mortals (D&C 128:15, 18).

Q: Will Satan be allowed to tempt during the Millennium?
A: No.

> There are many among us who teach that the binding of **Satan** will be merely the binding which those dwelling on the earth will place upon him by their refusal to hear his enticings. This is not so. He **will not have the privilege during that period of time to tempt any man** (D&C 101:28). (Joseph Fielding Smith, *Church History and Modern Revelation*, 1:192. Quoted in *Doctrine and Covenants Student Manual*, 1981, p. 89.)

Q: Will there be any non-LDS people on earth during the Millennium?
A: Of course! There will be many "good and honorable people" who will not be burned.

Imagine how much missionary work will need to be done when the survivors of the Second Coming discover that the Savior is LDS!

Q: What will life be like during the Millennium?
A: There will be peace and paradise-like conditions everywhere.

> During the millennial era, . . . mortality as such will continue. Children will be born, grow up, marry, advance to old age, and pass

> through the equivalent of death. Crops will be planted, harvested, and eaten; industries will be expanded, cities built, and education fostered; men will continue to care for their own needs, handle their own affairs, and enjoy the full endowment of . . . agency. Speaking a pure language (Zephaniah 3:9), dwelling in peace, living without disease. (Bruce R. McConkie, *Mormon Doctrine*, 1966, pp. 496–97)

Q: Will there be peace in the animal kingdom during the Millennium?

A: Yes, complete.

> Isaiah 11:6–9
>
> 6 The wolf also shall dwell with the lamb, and the leopard shall lie down with the kid [*young goat*]; and the calf and the young lion and the fatling together; and a little child shall lead them.
>
> 7 And the cow and the bear shall feed; their young ones shall lie down together: and the lion shall eat straw like the ox.
>
> 8 And the sucking child shall play on the hole of the asp [*viper*], and the weaned child shall put his hand on the cockatrice' [*venomous serpent*] den.
>
> 9 **They shall not hurt nor destroy in all my holy mountain**: for the earth shall be full of the knowledge of the LORD, as the waters cover the sea.

Q: What is the main work to be accomplished during the Millennium?

A: Missionary work and temple work.

There will be a tremendous need for missionary work as the Millennium gets under way. Just think of all the good and honorable people throughout the world who were not destroyed at the time of the Second Coming and who now will become aware of the fact that the Savior is LDS! Almost of them will want to be taught the gospel so they can join the Church and be saved.

Also, think of all the people from the time of Adam and Eve to the present who have been taught the gospel in the postmortal spirit world but whose names could not be found through family history research. Consequently, no temple work was done for them. Now, during the Millennium, their ordinance work can be done for them by mortal members of the Church, including marriages and sealing families together. By the way, all work for the dead must be done by mortals, according to Heavenly Father's great plan of salvation for His children. This was made clear in a revelation given through Joseph Smith.

D&C 128:15

15 And now, my dearly beloved brethren and sisters, let me assure you that these are principles in relation to the dead and the living that cannot be lightly passed over, as pertaining to our salvation. **For their salvation is necessary and essential to our salvation**, as Paul says concerning the fathers—that **they without us cannot be made perfect**—neither can we without our dead be made perfect.

Q: How old will people live to be during the Millennium?
A: One hundred years old.

Isaiah 65:20

20 There shall be no more thence an infant of days, nor an old man that hath not filled his days: for the child shall die an **hundred years old**; but the sinner *being* an hundred years old shall be accursed.

An institute of religion student manual has another good quote on the subject of how long mortals will live during the Millennium:

Men shall die when they are one hundred years of age, and the change shall be made suddenly to the immortal state. (*Doctrines of the Gospel Student Manual*, Religion 430 and 431, 2004, p. 104)

Q: What if the Millennium comes before I am married?
A: No problem. People can marry, have children, and enjoy all the blessings of family life during the Millennium.

Go back to the quote given after the question "What will life be like during the Millennium?" One real advantage to dating and marrying during the Millennium is that you can only date good people, because all the wicked were removed from the earth at the Second Coming.

Q: Is it true that during the Millennium righteous mothers will get to raise their little children who died during their life on earth before the Millennium?

A: Yes. And, of course, this includes righteous fathers, because this privilege is reserved for parents who are sealed together eternally.

> Joseph Smith declared that the mother who laid down her little child, being deprived of the privilege, the joy, and the satisfaction of bringing it up to manhood or womanhood in this world, would, after the resurrection, have all the joy, satisfaction and pleasure, and even more than it would have been possible to have had in mortality, in seeing her child grow to the full measure of the stature of its spirit. (Joseph F. Smith, *Gospel Doctrine*, Deseret Book, 1977, p. 453)

Q: Do mortals actually die during the Millennium, after they've lived to be one hundred?

A: Yes. But they will be resurrected immediately.

> D&C 101:31
>
> 31 And **when he dies** he shall not sleep, that is to say in the earth, but shall be **changed in the twinkling of an eye,** and shall be caught up, and his rest shall be glorious.

THE LITTLE SEASON—BATTLE OF GOG AND MAGOG

At the end of the thousand-year Millennium, we will have what the scriptures refer to as a "little season." During this time, the war, known as the "War in Heaven," which began clear back in premortality when Satan rebelled, and is continuing on earth now, will be brought to an end. It is a war for our souls.

Remember that Satan and his evil hosts were "bound" during the

Millennium and not allowed to tempt people on earth as they accomplished the work of the Lord during the thousand years of peace. Now, at the end of the Millennium, many mortals on earth will reject the Savior, whom they know personally, because they have seen Him since He has served as "King of kings" (Revelation 17:14) over all the earth. They will reject Christ's millennial teachings and ministry and will turn to wickedness. Satan and his evil hosts will be turned loose from being bound during the thousand years. Michael (Adam) will gather the armies of the righteous, and the devil will gather his armies for the final battle, usually referred to as the Battle of Gog and Magog. (See Bible Dictionary under "Gog.")

Satan and his evil followers will ultimately be defeated and cast out. This final scene, beginning with the releasing of Satan at the end of the Millennium, is described in the Doctrine and Covenants.

<u>D&C 88:111–15</u>

111 And then **he shall be loosed for a little season**, **that he may gather together his armies**.

112 And **Michael** [*Adam*], the seventh angel, even the archangel, **shall gather together his armies, even the hosts of heaven**.

113 And **the devil shall gather together his armies; even the hosts of hell, and shall come up to battle against Michael and his armies**.

114 And then cometh the battle of the great God; **and the devil and his armies shall be cast away into their own place** [*perdition, often referred to as "outer darkness"*], that **they shall not have power over the saints any more at all**.

115 For **Michael shall fight their battles, and shall overcome him** [*Satan and his followers*] who seeketh the throne of him [*Christ*] who sitteth upon the throne, even the Lamb.

We don't know how long this "little season" will last, but you can imagine what a great relief it will be for the righteous when the devil and the evil spirits who followed him in premortality and were cast out of heaven with him, as well as those mortals who have become sons of perdition, are permanently gone, "cast away into their own place." (See D&C 88:114.)

FINAL JUDGMENT

Have you ever wondered why this is called the final judgment? The reason is that by this time in Heavenly Father's outlined path to salvation for us, we will have gone through several partial judgments. For example, the "judgment" as to whether we went with Satan and the one third (Revelation 12:4) who were cast out with him, or we were allowed to come to earth to be born. Another partial judgment is when we die and go to the postmortal spirit world, whether we go to paradise or prison (Alma 40:12–13). Yet another judgment is when we are resurrected. We will get the type of resurrected body that belongs to celestial glory, terrestrial glory, telestial glory, or perdition (D&C 88:28–32.) So, we will know at the time we are resurrected which of the three degrees of glory or perdition we will go to. Final judgment will give the final details of our judgment, for example, whether we get the bottom, middle, or highest degree of the celestial kingdom (D&C 131:1–4.)

THREE DEGREES OF GLORY

The scriptures teach us that what most Christians refer to as heaven is actually divided up into three main categories. The Apostle Paul mentions these in the New Testament.

> 1 Corinthians 15:40–41
>
> 40 *There are* also **celestial** bodies, and bodies **terrestrial**: [*the* JST *adds "and bodies telestial"*] but the glory of the celestial *is* one, and the *glory* of the terrestrial *is* another [JST *"and the telestial, another"*].
>
> 41 ***There is* one glory of the sun** [*celestial kingdom*], and **another glory of the moon** [*terrestrial kingdom*], and **another glory of the stars** [*telestial kingdom*]: for *one* star differeth from *another* star in glory.

CELESTIAL KINGDOM

The celestial kingdom is where baptized members of the Church go, who honestly strive to be faithful to the gospel (D&C 76:50–53, 70). Babies and little children who die before the age of accountability also go to this kingdom (D&C 137:10). All the faithful, who will have ever lived on earth up to the last person born by the end of all things in preparation for the final judgment, who lived beyond the age of accountability (eight years old—D&C 68:27), who accepted and lived the gospel either on earth, in the postmortal spirit world mission field (spirit prison), or during the Millennium or the final windup scenes before the final judgment, who received their own ordinances or whose ordinance work was done by mortals, will obtain celestial glory. They will live with God and Christ in celestial splendor forever.

EXALTATION

The celestial kingdom has three degrees or categories. Families whose faithful members were sealed together on earth or through ordinance work for them after they died, will be in the highest degree of the celestial kingdom. This is called exaltation. It is also referred to in the scriptures as eternal life. It is the kind of life our Heavenly Parents live. This is the major goal of the entire gospel of Jesus Christ! It is the focus of the scriptures and everything we are taught by the Lord's prophets. Those who attain exaltation are described in Doctrine and Covenants 76:54–70, 131:1–4, and 132:19–20. There is no comparison between the blessings and benefits given to those who earn exaltation and those in any other category.

Those who obtain the other two degrees of the celestial kingdom will be separate and single but still have the blessing of living in the presence of God and Christ.

D&C 132:17

17 For these angels did not abide my law [*of celestial marriage*]; therefore, they cannot be enlarged [*cannot become gods*], but **remain separately and singly, without exaltation**, in their saved condition, to all eternity; and from henceforth are not gods, but are angels of God forever and ever.

Q: Will children who die before the years of accountability be exalted?

A: Yes.

Speaking of these children, President Joseph F. Smith taught,

> Under these circumstances, our beloved friends who are now deprived of their little one, have great cause for joy and rejoicing, even in the midst of the deep sorrow that they feel at the loss of their little one for a time. They know he is all right; they have the assurance that their little one has passed away without sin. Such children are in the bosom of the Father. **They will inherit their glory and their exaltation.** (*Gospel Doctrine*, President Joseph F. Smith, Deseret Book, 1977, p. 453)

Q: How can such children obtain exaltation, since they are not married in the temple?

A: They will get married by proxy in a temple during the Millennium.

Children who die before the years of accountability are full-grown spirits when they die and go to paradise in the postmortal spirit world. There or during the Millennium, they can date, grow in love, and, during the Millennium, the couple can present themselves in a temple to be married by proxy for time and all eternity. Thus, they fully qualify for exaltation on judgment day.

Q: What about the righteous who wanted to marry but died without getting a fair chance for temple marriage during mortality or whose temple marriage did not work out?

A: All will have a completely fair chance to marry for time and eternity, either in this life or through missionary work in the spirit world and ordinances performed for the dead in temples, including during the Millennium. In other words, all will have a completely fair opportunity for the blessings of eternal marriage before the final judgment.

> We promise you that insofar as eternity is concerned, no soul will be deprived of rich and high and eternal blessings for anything which that person could not help, that the Lord never fails in his promises, and that every righteous person will receive eventually all to which the person is entitled and which he or she has not forfeited through any fault of his or her own. (President Spencer W. Kimball, "The Importance of Celestial Marriage," *Ensign*, October 1979, p. 5)

Q: Do we, as members of the Church, have to be pretty much perfect when we die, in order to obtain exaltation on Judgment Day?

A: No. But we do need to be on the path toward that goal.

> Another idea that is powerful to lift us from discouragement is that the work of the Church . . . is an eternal work. Not all problems . . . are fixed in mortality. The work of salvation goes on beyond the veil of death, and we should not be too apprehensive about incompleteness within the limits of mortality. (Dallin H. Oaks, "Powerful Ideas," *Ensign*, November 1995, p. 26)

> I am also convinced of the fact that **the speed with which we head along the straight and narrow path isn't as important as the direction in which we are traveling**. That direction, if it is leading toward eternal goals, is the all-important factor. (Marvin J. Ashton, "On Being Worthy," *Ensign*, May 1989, 21; April 1989 General Conference)

TERRESTRIAL KINGDOM

Those who go to the terrestrial kingdom will be good and honorable people who choose not to fully embrace and live the gospel. They will avoid sexual immorality, dishonesty, murder, and other sins that would take people to telestial glory. As far as we know, there is only one kingdom or category in terrestrial glory. You can read about this kingdom in Doctrine and Covenants 76:71–79.

TELESTIAL KINGDOM

Those who go to the telestial kingdom are those who fall into the category of being truly wicked but do not deny the Holy Ghost (which would make them sons of perdition). Some lifestyles that would lead to being assigned to telestial glory are described as follows:

D&C 76:103

103 These are they who are **liars,** and **sorcerers** [*those deeply involved in the occult*], and **adulterers**, and **whoremongers** [*people who make illicit sex the central focus of their lives*], and **whosoever loves and makes a lie** [*including those who are involved in sexual immorality and lie to attempt to cover it up*].

The Book of Revelation adds another major category for this kingdom:

Revelation 22:15

15 For without *are* dogs [*male prostitutes*], and sorcerers, and whoremongers, and **murderers**, and idolaters, and whosoever loveth and maketh a lie.

The Apostle Paul further describes sins that could lead to telestial glory.

Galatians 5:19–21

19 Now the works of the flesh are manifest, which are *these* [*now here are some of the worldly sins you must avoid*]; **Adultery**, **fornication**, **uncleanness**, **lasciviousness** [*lustful thinking and talking and all sexual immorality, including pornography*],

20 **Idolatry** [*idol worship*], **witchcraft**, **hatred**, **variance** [*disharmony*], **emulations** [*rivalry, etc., based on jealousy and worldly ambitions*], **wrath** [*anger, loss of temper*]**, strife**, **seditions** [*stirring up unrighteous discontent with those in power, including government leaders and Church leaders*], **heresies** [*false doctrines*],

21 **Envyings**, **murders**, **drunkenness**, **revellings** [*riotous, drunken parties and lifestyles*], and such like: of the which I tell you before [*I forewarn you*], as I have also told *you* in time past, that **they which do such things shall not inherit the kingdom of God** [*the celestial kingdom, nor terrestrial for that matter*].

You can find more about the telestial kingdom and who goes there in Doctrine and Covenants 76:81–89 and 98–102. It is interesting to see in the scriptures that even this degree of glory is so wonderful that we can't even imagine it. This is a reminder of the love that God has for His children.

D&C 76:89

89 And thus we saw, in the heavenly vision, **the glory of the telestial**, which **surpasses all understanding**.

PERDITION (OUTER DARKNESS)

Those who will be assigned to perdition, or what we sometimes refer to as "outer darkness," include the one third who followed Satan during the War in Heaven (Revelation 12:4) and were cast out with him (Revelation 12:7–9.) Also, in this category, will be mortals who retrogress to the point that they literally become like Satan. They agree with him in every point. They hate righteousness like he does. They hate God and Christ like he does. They think like he does, defy and fight against the true Church like he does, laugh and rejoice when people are tortured and killed like he does (3 Nephi 9:2), and want everyone to be miserable like he does (2 Nephi 2:27). In short, they become completely and irrevocably wicked, in total opposition to God, and have absolutely not the slightest inclination at all to repent and change from being devils. Fortunately, this is impossible for most of us to even conceive of because of the mercy that lives within our souls and the benefit of the doubt for others that is inspired by the Holy Ghost in us. But it is true. They are completely out of reach of the Atonement by their own choice.

The Doctrine and Covenants describes sons of perdition:

D&C 76:30–36

30 And we saw a vision of the sufferings of those with whom he [*Satan*] made war and overcame, for thus came the voice of the Lord unto us:

31 Thus saith the Lord concerning **all those who know my power** [*have a strong testimony from the Holy Ghost*], and **have been made partakers thereof** [*have received baptism, confirmation, and temple ordinances*], and suffered [*allowed*] themselves through the power of the devil to be overcome, and to **deny the truth** [*lie about what they know is true*] **and defy my power** [*fight against the Church and God*]—

32 **They are** they who are the **sons of perdition**, of whom I say that it had been better for them never to have been born;

33 For **they are vessels of wrath** [*filled with satanic anger and rage against good*], doomed to suffer the wrath of God, with the devil and his angels in eternity;

34 Concerning whom I have said there is **no forgiveness** in this world nor in the world to come—

35 Having **denied the Holy Spirit after having received it**, and having **denied the Only Begotten Son** of the Father, **having crucified him unto themselves and put him to an open shame** [*would gladly crucify Christ again and subject Him to ridicule, if they could*].

36 **These are they who shall go** away into the lake of fire and brimstone, **with the devil and his angels**—

Q: Can both men and women become sons of perdition?
A: Yes, according to Brigham Young.

How much does it take to prepare a man, or woman . . . to become angels to the devil, to suffer with him through all eternity? Just as much as it does to prepare a man to go into the Celestial Kingdom, into the presence of the Father and the Son, and to be made an heir to his kingdom and all his glory, and be crowned with crowns of glory, immortality, and eternal lives. (Brigham Young, *Journal of Discourses*, Vol. 3, p. 93)

THEN WHAT?

Many members of the Church get to this point in their study of the plan of salvation, or, in other words, to the end of Judgment Day and to being assigned to one of the three degrees of glory or perdition and then stop. The answer to "Then what?" is really what it's all about. It's the whole and wonderful answer to why we strive to be obedient and live the gospel.

Here's the answer to "Then what?" Those who attain exaltation in the celestial kingdom will continue living in their own family units. They will continue progressing until they become gods. They will be blessed to live the happiest and most satisfying lifestyle of all in the universe, the same as our Heavenly Parents live. They will have spirit offspring, their own spirit children, and, as needed, will create worlds for them on which they can be born, obtain physical bodies, be taught the gospel, and go through all of the steps and phases of the plan of salvation we are now going through in our quest for exaltation.

> Only resurrected and glorified beings can become parents of spirit offspring. Only such exalted souls have reached maturity in the appointed course of eternal life; and **the spirits born to them in the eternal worlds will pass in due sequence through the several stages or estates by which the glorified parents have attained exaltation**. (First Presidency Statement, *Improvement Era*, August 1916, p. 942)

In other words, if we become gods, we will use the same plan of salvation for our own spirit children as was used for us.

Q: Have any normal mortals from this world become gods yet?
A: Yes

Abraham, Isaac, and Jacob (and their faithful wives, of course) have already become gods.

<u>D&C 132:29, 37</u>

29 **Abraham** received all things, whatsoever he received, by revelation and commandment, by my word, saith the Lord, and **hath entered into his exaltation and sitteth upon his throne**.

37 **Abraham** received concubines, and they bore him children; and it was accounted unto him for righteousness, because they were given unto him, and he abode in my law; as **Isaac** also and **Jacob** did none other things than that which they were commanded; and because they did none other things than that which they were commanded, they **have entered into their exaltation**, according to the promises, **and sit upon thrones, and are not angels but are gods**.

7

IN CONCLUSION

As you prepare yourself to understand and teach the plan of salvation, which is the "big picture" that gives meaning and eternal context to everything we do in life, you are preparing yourself to be a more effective missionary during your formal mission and during your entire life as a servant of God. You are preparing even now to help friends and family to better understand the Father's plan and purposes for them. You are preparing to be more effective as a parent as you teach the gospel in your own future home. And finally, you are preparing yourself to be more firmly anchored to the iron rod as you continue with your own precious gifts of life and moral agency, given you by your loving Heavenly Father.

PERSONAL NOTES

PERSONAL NOTES

PERSONAL NOTES

PERSONAL NOTES

ABOUT THE AUTHOR

David J. Ridges taught for the Church Educational System for thirty-five years. He taught adult religion and Know Your Religion classes for BYU Continuing Education and spoke at BYU Campus Education Week for many years. He has served as a curriculum writer for Sunday School, seminary, and institute of religion manuals. His callings in the Church include Gospel Doctrine teacher, bishop, stake president, and patriarch. He and his wife, Janette, have served two full-time Church Educational System missions. They are the parents of six children and are enjoying a growing number of grandchildren. They reside in Springville, Utah.